An author of walking and travel books, Peter Caton has walked on Dartmoor for more than 50 years. He has an extensive knowledge of the moors, their history, legends and many places of interest.

WALKS
DISCOVERING LESSER KNOWN DARTMOOR

Peter Caton

Copyright © 2022 Peter Caton
Reprinted 2023

The moral right of the author has been asserted.

Apart from any fair dealing for the purposes of research or private study, or criticism or review, as permitted under the Copyright, Designs and Patents Act 1988, this publication may only be reproduced, stored or transmitted, in any form or by any means, with the prior permission in writing of the publishers, or in the case of reprographic reproduction in accordance with the terms of licences issued by the Copyright Licensing Agency. Enquiries concerning reproduction outside those terms should be sent to the publishers.

Matador
Unit E2 Airfield Business Park,
Harrison Road, Market Harborough,
Leicestershire. LE16 7UL
Tel: 0116 2792299
Email: books@troubador.co.uk
Web: www.troubador.co.uk/matador
Twitter: @matadorbooks

ISBN 978 1803132 303

British Library Cataloguing in Publication Data.
A catalogue record for this book is available from the British Library.

Printed and bound by CPI Group (UK) Ltd, Croydon, CR0 4YY
Typeset in 11pt Gill Sans by Troubador Publishing Ltd, Leicester, UK
Maps produced by Location Maps Ltd.
Cover Photo – Teign-e-ver Clapper Bridge

Matador is an imprint of Troubador Publishing Ltd

To my father, Michael Caton, who introduced me to Dartmoor and whose help, knowledge and enthusiasm for the moor has been of huge assistance and inspiration in the writing of this book.

The author is always pleased to hear from
readers through his website:

www.petercatonbooks.co.uk

Twitter – @petercatonbooks
Facebook – Peter Caton Books

The Walks

Many of the walks have two or three options. In most cases the B & C options also include the points of interest in Walk A.

Walk	Start Miles	Ease	Visits
1A	Sourton 2½	*	Sourton Tors Ice Works, Cider Press, Stone Circle
1B	Sourton 7½	***	Rattlebrook Railway, Bleak House
2A	Meldon 4½	**	Meldon Reservoir, Island of Rocks, Black-a-Tor Copse
2B	Meldon 5 / 7	***	Black Tor
3A	Okehampton Stn. / Camp 3 / 5½	*	Fitz's Well, Black Down Target Railway, Red-a-ven Dip
3B	Okehampton Stn. / Camp 4 / 6½	**	Red-a-ven Valley, Meldon Mine
4	Belstone 3½	*	Belstone, Cullever Steps, Irishman's Wall, Nine Maidens

5A	Scorhill Farm 7½	***	Buttern Hill Stone Circle, Wild Tor, Watern Combe, Watern Tor
5B	Scorhill Farm 6½	****	Returns by River Teign
6	Batworthy 3 / 3½	*	Scorhill Circle, Teign-e-ver Clapper, Tolmen Stone, Shovel Down
7A	Fernworthy 2½	*	Fernworthy Reservoir Circuit
7B	Fernworthy 7	**	Froggymead Stone Circle, Teignhead Farm, Manga Brook Waterfall, Manga Farm
8	Warren House Inn 3 / 3½	**	Hurston Ridge Stone Row, Bennett's Cross, Vitifer Mine
9	Shapley Common Car Park 4	*	Shapley Tor, Hookney Tor, Grimspound
10	Dunstone Down 1½	*	Wind Tor, Hutholes
11	Haytor Visitor Centre 2½ / 3¼	*	Haytor Quarry, Granite Tramway, Quarrymen's Hut

THE WALKS

12	Cold East Cross Car Park 2	*	Buckland Beacon, Welstor Common
13	Venford Reservoir 1½	****	River Dart, Venford Falls
14A	Cross Furzes 5 / 4	*	Huntingdon Warren
14B	Cross Furzes 6 / 5	***	Huntingdon Chapel & Cross
14C	Cross Furzes 7	***	Broad Falls, Huntingdon Clapper
15A	Shipley Bridge 3½	**	Diamond Lane, Corringdon Ball Tomb, Stone Rows
15B	Shipley Bridge 7½	***	Three Barrows, Knattabarrow Pool, Zeal Tramway
16	Ivybridge Station 6½	**	Spurrell's Cross, Cuckoo Ball Burial Chamber
17A	Harford 4	*	Spurrell's Cross, The Longstone, Butterdon Stone Row
17B	Harford / Ivybridge 6½ / 8	*	Black Pool & Western Beacon
18A	Harford / Ivybridge 5½ / 11	**	Stalldown Stone Row, Hillson's House

18B	Harford / Ivybridge 6½ / 12	***	Downing's House
19	Nr. Cadover Bridge 5½	***	The Bandstand, Shavercombe Waterfall
20A	Norsworthy Bridge 3½	*	Devonport Leat & Black Tor Falls
20B	Norsworthy Bridge 4½	**	Crazywell Pool, Cross & Farm
20C	Norsworthy Bridge 8½	**	Nun's Cross & Farm, Monks' Path & Crosses
21	Four Winds Car Park 1½	*	Merrivale
22A	Lane End 2¼ / 3¼	**	Lower Tavy Cleave & Ger Ter
22B	Lane End 5	****	Tavy Cleave, Rattle Brook, Wheel Pit, Hare Tor
23A	Princetown 4	*	Princetown Railway & Foggintor Quarry
23B	Princetown 8	*	Swell Tor & Ingra Tor Quarries
24	Princetown 3¾	*	Conchie Road, Crock of Gold
25A	Nr. Whiteworks 4½	**	Childe's Tomb, Fox Tor, Nuns Cross Farm & Cross

THE WALKS

25B	Nr. Whiteworks 8½	****	Black Lane, Ducks' Pool, Phillpotts' Cave
25C	Nr. Whiteworks 2	*	Nuns Cross Farm & Cross
26A	Two Bridges 5	**	Beardown Tors, Devonport Leat
26B	Two Bridges 4½	**	Beardown Tors, Wistman's Wood
26C	Two Bridges 8	****	Beardown Man, Browns House
27A	Postbridge 4 / 5	**	Roundy Park Cist, Waterfall, Beehive Hut
27B	Postbridge 6 / 7	**	Sandy Hole Pass

*	Easy
**	Fairly easy
***	Moderate
****	Challenging

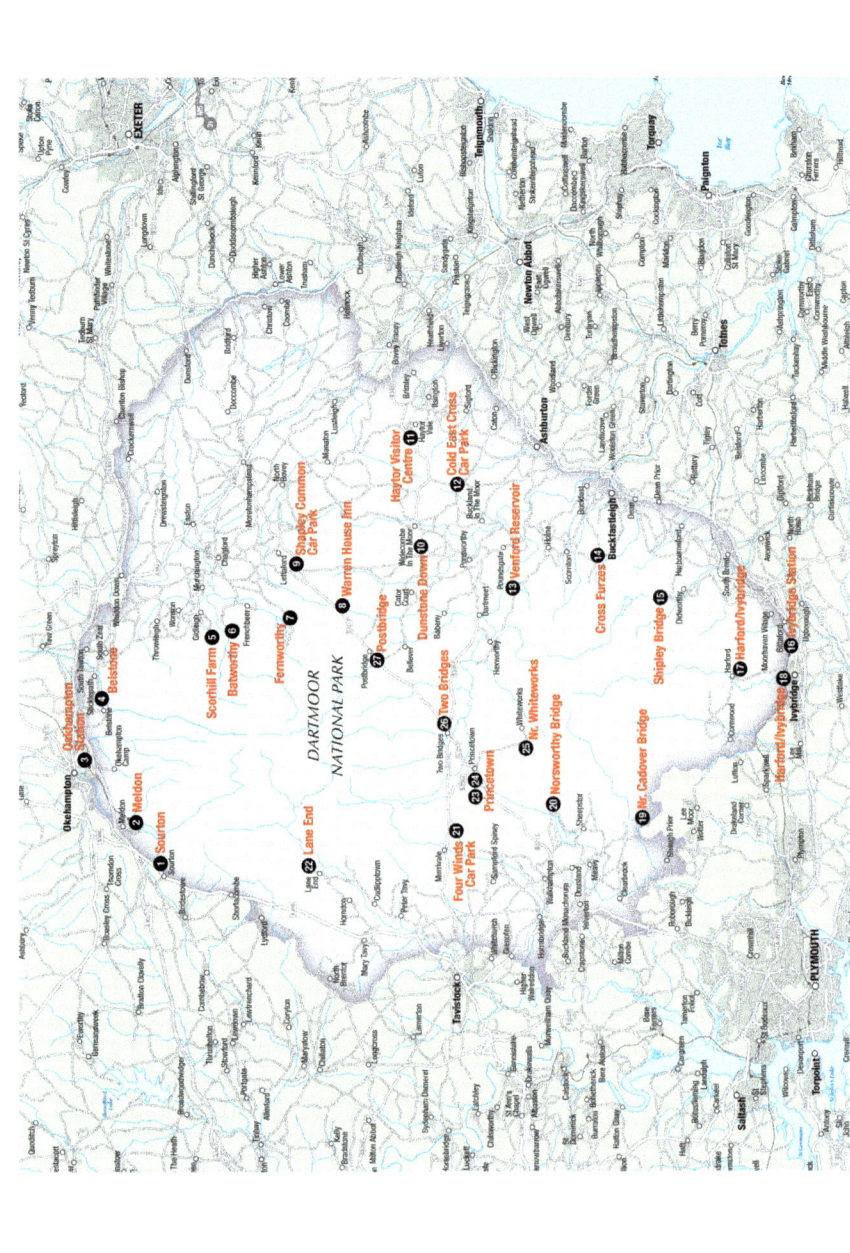

Introduction

The wildest, most remote and arguably the most beautiful area in Southern England, Dartmoor attracts many visitors. Some visit just a few of the well known 'honeypot' sites such as Haytor and Dartmeet. Others are experienced Dartmoor walkers who need little help to plan walks and find their way across the moor. In this book I have aimed to cater for the visitors who want to walk away from the crowds, discover more of the beauty of Dartmoor and find some of its lesser known sites of interest.

There are many walking guides but I've tried to make this one a little different. It covers a range of walks, from short strolls on easy paths, to challenging walks into the heart of the moor, with the aim to take the walker to some of Dartmoor's lesser known places of historical interest or beauty. I have given more information on the places visited than in most walking guides, as well as a comprehensive introduction to the moor.

The walks will take you to antiquities dating from the Bronze Age or even earlier, to hidden waterfalls and gorges, abandoned remote dwellings, fascinating industrial archaeology, interesting tors and wonderful viewpoints. For those who don't know Dartmoor they provide ideas for interesting walks of varying length and difficulty. Whilst some of the points of interest will be familiar to those who know the moor well, the walks will take you to places that very few people visit, passing little known artefacts and I hope there will be something new for almost everyone.

The walks don't have to be followed in their entirety. They can be cut short or just some sections selected and still see places of interest but with easier walking if preferred. Some chapters cover two or three options (A, B, C), often of different length or difficulty, and in these the routes B & C mostly include the places visited in A. Most walks are circular but if difficult ground or lack of paths make this less easy I have shown linear routes, although of course the views are different in reverse.

Each walk is accompanied with a map, to be used in conjunction with the directions, however an Ordnance Survey or Harvey's British Mountain Map covering the wider area should also be carried. Distances are shown in miles, as this is what most walkers use (to confirm I ran a survey on a ramblers' Facebook group and 90% preferred miles), hence to avoid mixing units I've used the traditional yards not metres. Most distances are shown as approximate but should you wish to convert, a mile is 1.6 km and 100 yards is roughly 90 metres. When describing monuments, rather than converting, I've used the units stated in my sources, hence there is a mix of metric and imperial.

The instructions are as detailed as reasonably practical without mentioning every bend or side path. Walkers should assume that the route stays on the same path or track, not taking turnings to left or right, unless stated. Dartmoor is a wild place and the centre of it can truly be described as a wilderness. There are paths and tracks and I've used these where possible but some walks include more challenging sections over rougher moorland. Some paths are more permanent than others and the ease of finding or following them can depend on the time of year and state of vegetation.

Sometimes maps show paths that may not exist or an incorrect alignment, but conversely there are many paths that aren't included on most maps. Ordnance Survey and British Mountain Maps do not always agree and one may show useful information that is not on the other. Grid references are included for most points of interest. Departing from the convention, which can be confusing, when describing routes by rivers I have used left / right from the direction one is facing, rather than always with the direction of flow. Many places on Dartmoor are known by more than one name. To avoid confusion I've generally used the version shown on OS maps but also mentioned some of the older or locally used names.

Dartmoor's paths are often not the easy footpaths one might follow through fields or along the coast. Sometimes they define a route but it can be necessary to pick the best way through boulders

INTRODUCTION

or marshy areas. Where practical I have indicated the type of path and whether it is 'patchy'. There is no clear division between a path and a track but as a general rule if it can be used by farm vehicles I have referred to it as a track. Sometimes one can follow the many sheep paths that wander across the moor.

To indicate the level of difficulty I've rated each walk on a scale of one to four, based on the availability of paths, ease of going and need for navigational skills, rather than length:

*	Easy walk on good paths.
**	Fairly easy walk. May have short sections on rougher ground or without clear paths.
***	Moderate walk. Some stretches without paths. May have some rough or boggy ground.
****	Challenging walk over rocks and / or potentially rough / boggy ground, or into centre of the moor where good navigation skills are essential.

Of course one person's challenging walk may seem easy to an experienced Dartmoor walker, however this should act as a rough guide. Being moorland one can expect some gradients but if there are particularly steep climbs I've mentioned this in the text. Note too that the weather is a factor and that all walks are more difficult in strong wind, rain or mist. The walks, particularly the three and four star walks, should not be attempted unless you are competent at using a map and compass, especially if there is any risk of mist or poor weather. Whilst Dartmoor is magical in snow, I would not recommend venturing far if the ground is covered. It is strongly recommended that to get an idea of the route and terrain and to learn what to look out for, you read through the walk before setting off.

The walks are spread across the whole of Dartmoor and arranged roughly clockwise around the moor, followed by those starting closer to the centre. They all start from points where cars can be parked and grid references for these are shown. At busy times car parks can become full and it is best to arrive early to ensure a spot in the smaller areas. Some can be reached by the limited bus routes that serve Dartmoor, although this may require a longish walk from the nearest village. I have included walks from the two railway stations serving Dartmoor; Ivybridge and Okehampton. Information on refreshments, charges and toilet availability at the car parks is believed to be correct at the time of publication but may change over time.

I have carefully considered and taken opinions from others as to whether some of Dartmoor's lesser known places should be publicised. There is a view that they should be kept secret for the locals, but it seems to me reasonable that the beauty of the moor and its places of interest should be shared. There's also an argument that it's best to spread people round the moor but in any case this book won't make a huge difference. At a very rough calculation based on 3,000 copies sold and every reader doing four walks a year, each walk will be followed about once a day. Of course some will be more popular and some days will be busier than others but it is still unlikely that your solitude at any one point will be interrupted as a result of others following the book.

The book includes background information on the history, legends and stories associated with various places visited in the walks. Some of this I have gained or confirmed from books listed in the bibliography. Also from various websites. I would particularly mention *www.legendarydartmoor.co.uk*, which has extensive information on many of Dartmoor's legends, and *www.dartefacts.co.uk*, a database of Dartmoor artefacts. The Facebook group **Dartmoor 365** has also been helpful. Where sources contradict I have either stated this or gone with what I consider to be the most reliable version.

Dartmoor is a wild place and whilst serious incidents are relatively rare, there is potential for getting into problems when walking. The sections on military firing and safety should be read by anyone embarking on these walks and the specific warnings shown with some walks heeded.

Whilst it is right to highlight safety and that walking on Dartmoor is not the same as a local country park, visitors should not be put off, but ensure that they take adequate care and remain within their

INTRODUCTION

capabilities. Walking on Dartmoor is a wonderful experience and I hope that this book will help introduce those of all ages and abilities to places they may not otherwise have found.

Dartmoor's History

Around 300 million years ago magma forced up through the Earth's crust cooled to create the granite which is so characteristic of Dartmoor, but the moor as we know it has been formed as a result of natural erosion and the activities of people.

Weathering exposed the granite on hill tops, forming the iconic tors and rivers cut its valleys. Trees, which covered most of Dartmoor following the last Ice Age, were gradually removed by early settlers and blanket peat bog formed on much of the higher moor.

In the Mesolithic Period (10,000–4000 BC) small groups of hunter-gatherers searched the forests for food but left little trace other than their stone tools. Neolithic people lived around, but probably not actually on Dartmoor, from about 4000–2500 BC and started limited farming, beginning the process of tree clearance and leaving some remains, mainly tombs. It is however the Bronze Age period for which Dartmoor is most notable.

Most of the many prehistoric remains come from the Early Bronze Age (2500–1700 BC), when stone rows, stone circles and burial chambers were constructed. By Middle Bronze Age (1700–1200 BC) Dartmoor was fairly well populated, people living in huts, with land divided by reaves. From Late Bronze Age through to Roman times (1200 BC–410 AD) it seems that there was only scattered occupation of the moor, although Iron Age people built a number of hill forts around its edges.

Medieval villages grew up around Dartmoor, forming the basis of most current settlements and the moorland was exploited extensively for grazing and more latterly industrial uses. Tin extraction, initially harvesting alluvial deposits around streams, then digging open cast mines or shafts, had the biggest impact, with many remains and earthworks still visible. Tinning continued into the 20th century, as did mining for other minerals, including china clay extraction which is still active on the western edge of the moor. Granite has been quarried and peat cut, with tracks and railways built across the moor to service its industries.

Farming has shaped Dartmoor and continues to do so. If the moor was not grazed its character would soon change. In medieval times people from across Devon used Dartmoor for summer grazing of livestock and crops were grown around the fringes. Victorians built remote farms, some of which still stand, but efforts to improve the land using modern techniques largely failed and most were abandoned. Rabbit warrening was carried out extensively until well into the 20th century.

In Victorian times our countryside began to be viewed with a new perspective and Dartmoor became valued for its beauty and history, not just as a foreboding place visited only by those who had to work here. People started to travel to the moor for pleasure, with tourism and walking becoming popular. This brought new conflicts, with conservationists wanting to keep Dartmoor as an unspoilt wilderness, objecting to military use and damage from industry.

The Dartmoor Preservation Association (DPA) was formed in 1883 and battles have been fought over reservoirs, china clay extraction, forestation and other developments. National Park status was granted in 1951 but there are still conflicts on a moor where people live and farm, but with so many antiquities to preserve and a unique environment that people wish to visit and enjoy.

Wildlife

The peat moorland and wooded valleys which surround it provide varied habitats for flora and fauna, including many rare species.

Otters may be spotted by Dartmoor's rivers, where salmon and trout spawn. Leats contain good populations of small trout and herons are seen waiting patiently to catch a passing fish.

Skylark, snipe, ring ouzel and cuckoo thrive on the open moor, where there are internationally important populations of meadow pipit and stonechat. Buzzards are often seen soaring above the moor.

Common lizards and adders can be seen sunning themselves in warm spots or scuttling off after being disturbed. Adder bites are rare but should you be bitten seek medical help immediately. Dartmoor is also home to the ash black, the world's largest land slug.

The famous Dartmoor ponies are not wild but are owned by Dartmoor commoners, locals who have grazing rights on the moor. The ponies play a vital role in maintaining habitats but should not be approached closely or fed.

Dartmoor is particularly important for its rare insects, including southern damselfly, marsh fritillary butterfly, narrow-bordered bee hawkmoth and bog hoverfly. The ancient oak woodlands are the only place in the world where the Heckford pigmy moth can be found.

More than 120 types of lichen are found in Dartmoor's ancient woods and 60 on its granite tors. Rare lichens grow particularly on rocks rich in heavy metals which were exposed by mining.

Plants of note include heathers, which colour much of the moor purple in summer and autumn, gorse with its bright yellow flowers and in miry areas, sphagnum moss, cotton grass and bog asphodel. Whortleberries, small black berries, grow on low bushes often amongst granite rocks. Also known as 'hurts' on Dartmoor and 'bilberries' elsewhere, these edible berries were once extensively harvested and can still be picked for a snack by walkers.

Finally I should mention Dartmoor's most elusive residents, the pixies. Whilst rarely seen, they seem to be most commonly spotted by gentlemen returning home from an evening in a local hostelry. These cheeky chaps are generally friendly but get quite upset if offended and reputedly may mislead travellers, causing them to become disorientated and pixie-led. The solution to this is to turn one's coat inside out.

Dartmoor Features

Whilst sometimes parts of Dartmoor may appear to be a barren landscape, the moor is covered with a huge number of historical and physical features that add interest to our walks.

Physical Features

Tors – Probably the feature most associated with Dartmoor, these are huge granite rocks, mostly standing on the summits of hills. There are more than 160 named tors on Dartmoor.

Clitter – Smaller rocks which have been eroded from tors and often cover the slopes below the summit.

Rivers – With double the rainfall of Plymouth, most of Devon's rivers rise on the boggy high ground of Dartmoor. The majority of the fast-flowing streams and rivers flow south to the English Channel, whilst the Taw & Okements eventually reach Bideford Bay. Some streams on Dartmoor are called 'Lake'.

Waterfalls – Some of the most picturesque places on Dartmoor are where its rivers and streams cascade over granite boulders as they drop from the boggy highland into moorland valleys, or through woodland as they flow off the moor.

Bogs – Blanket bog, at least 50cm depth of peat formed from decayed sphagnum moss, covers much of central Dartmoor. It is of international significance, a carbon reservoir and a sponge which slowly releases water into the moor's rivers.

Prehistoric Features

Hut Circles – Low circular stone walls that were the base for conical wood or thatched roofs, used by Bronze Age people as homes and animal housing. There are several thousand on Dartmoor. Also known as round houses.

Pounds – Walled enclosures containing a number of hut circles, forming settlements for Bronze Age dwellers.

Reaves – Bronze Age boundaries of stone and earth, forming field and land boundaries.

INTRODUCTION

Stone Circles – Circles of stones typically 20 – 40 yards in diameter, dating from the Bronze Age. Their exact purpose is unknown but it is thought that they acted as ritual centres and maybe places of gathering. They may also have had astronomical uses, perhaps as a calendar mapping movement of sun, moon and stars.

Stone Rows – Roughly straight lines of standing stones (sometimes double or more parallel lines) extending from a few yards to a mile or more. They were constructed by Bronze Age people but their purpose is unknown. The approximately 75 stone rows on Dartmoor is more than half the total found in the whole UK.

Menhirs (Standing Stones) – Large upright stones either standing alone or forming the terminal stone of a stone row. Dating from the Bronze Age they are thought to be memorials, or to mark graves and they may also have been way markers.

Kistvaens (Cists / Kists) – Bronze Age stone burial chambers consisting of four sides, a capstone and occasionally a paved floor. Most were originally covered with earth or stone and nearly all are oriented in a NW / SE direction, maybe so that the deceased were laid facing the sun. There are around 200 on Dartmoor.

Cairns – Mounds of earth or stones, often on hill tops, covering Bronze Age burials. Common on Dartmoor.

Long Barrows – Also known as chambered tombs, these are Neolithic burial tombs consisting of earth mounds with a stone chamber at one end. Some have lost their mound over the centuries and most of the stone chambers have been damaged. Very few long barrows have been found on Dartmoor.

Sacred Pools – Shallow pools, often located between ridges. The regular circular or oval shapes suggest that they were constructed or modified by humans. The pools are thought to date from prehistoric times and many appear to be part of Bronze Age complexes, being close to cairns & stone rows. There may be around 40 on Dartmoor but some people dispute their origin.

Historic Features

Clapper Bridges – Bridges formed of granite slabs, either a single span resting on river banks, or a number of slabs standing on dry-stone piers. Many date from medieval times and are on the routes of old packhorse tracks, whilst others were erected more latterly by local farmers.

Leats – Artificial water courses supplying water to domestic, agricultural and industrial users. Some remain in use, although often not for their original purpose, whilst others are dry. Leats supplying water to farms were known as pot water leats.

Crosses – Stone crosses marking ancient tracks or routes, boundaries, or acting as memorials. Some are relatively modern but most date back hundreds of years.

Tinning Remains – Many remains from the extensive tin mining can be seen on the moor. Blowing houses, small stone buildings used for smelting tin, date from the 14th to 19th centuries. These contained a small blast furnace into which air was blown by bellows powered by a water wheel. The molten tin produced was poured into mould stones, some of which can be found in the remains of the more than 40 blowing houses identified on Dartmoor. Mortar stones, in which ore was crushed, are found within or close to blowing houses. Wheel pits, remains of buildings and shafts from more recent deep mines are seen in a number of sites across the moor.

Beehive Huts – Small stone huts used as stores or shelters by miners or quarrymen.

INTRODUCTION

Newtakes – Areas of moorland enclosed by drystone walls, mostly built in the 18th century when largely unsuccessful attempts were made to improve the land for agriculture.

Strolls / Stroles – Converging stone walls approaching moor gates, built to facilitate driving livestock from the moors. Both spellings are used.

Boundary Stones – Standing stones, often with inscribed letters, marking boundaries between parishes or land belonging to different owners.

Rabbit Warrens – Farms where rabbits were bred commercially for fur and meat. There were about 18 warrens on Dartmoor, which were active from the Middle Ages to the 20th century. Some warren houses still stand but most have been lost, however other remains such as pillow mounds (artificial burrows) and vermin traps can be seen.

Ancient Tracks – Various tracks cross Dartmoor, many of which date back centuries. Their origins varied and are the subject of legends but include use by traders, monks travelling between monasteries and even for carrying coffins over the moor to parish churches for burial.

Peat Passes – Passes dug into peat on High Northern Dartmoor to provide a way through boggy areas. Most were commissioned by the keen huntsman Frank Philpotts.

Quarrying Relics – Dressed granite, millstones, apple crushers etc. which have been abandoned on the moor.

Dartmoor Legends

One could easily fill a book with Dartmoor legends and consideration as to which may have a basis of truth in their origin. Most are associated with specific places on the moor and I've mentioned many in the texts of the walks.

Military Firing

Much of the moor is used by the military and there are three ranges on Northern Dartmoor where live firing takes place. At these times public access is banned and red flags (lights at night) are shown prominently around the range boundaries. Firing times are well publicised and can be seen online at *https://www.gov.uk/government/publications/dartmoor-firing-programme*.

Dartmoor has been used by the military since the early 1800s and unexploded ammunition could be found anywhere on the moor. Don't touch any suspicious metal objects and if you find anything that may be unexploded ordnance report it to Okehampton Camp, the police, or a National Park visitor centre.

Safety

With proper preparation, provided common sense is used, walking on Dartmoor should not be hazardous but it is a wild place, especially in the centre, and therefore vital that walkers are aware of the potential dangers. Particular risks to be aware of are getting lost, weather, bogs and accidents.

Parts of Dartmoor are quite featureless and it is easy to go the wrong way. The key to not getting badly lost is to always know where you are and stopping to assess the position rather than ploughing on regardless. A map and compass are essential – don't rely solely on GPS, phone signals or batteries.

Dartmoor's weather can change very rapidly. Check the forecast but always be prepared for sudden onset of rain or mist. Take particular care in winter but always carry plenty of warm clothing, including waterproofs. Appropriate footwear is essential. Mist can be disorientating and it is very easy to get lost. There is little shelter from rain or sun on the moor and often the best one can find is behind rocks in lee of the wind. The wind can be strong enough to blow a person off exposed tors. River levels can rise rapidly and sometimes a stream crossed easily on the outward walk can be a dangerous torrent by the return. Take great care crossing rivers. It is very easy to slip when jumping from a soft bank or stepping on wet rocks.

Many parts of High Dartmoor are blanket peat bog and whilst the worst areas should be avoided, there is a risk of sinking into a bog, especially if you lose your route. Should this happen, don't struggle or panic. The biggest risk is from stress, exhaustion or hypothermia, not being sucked under. If others are nearby get them to throw something to grab onto but make sure they don't get stuck too. The best way to escape is to slowly extricate one leg at a time, and if necessary spread yourself and snake out.

It is easy to turn an ankle or worse on Dartmoor's rough ground, although the risk is lessened by wearing good walking boots. Should you be injured by a fall, slip or putting your foot into a hole, or become ill, and are unable to walk off the moor, call the police who coordinate rescue services. They will require your exact location. If there is no mobile signal and other people are with you get someone to climb a hill where they will be more likely to make a call. If alone and unable to walk, use a whistle to attract help whilst trying to keep warm and dry. Consider carrying a personal locator beacon if walking alone in remote areas.

There are ticks on Dartmoor bringing the risk of Lyme disease. If walking through rough vegetation wear long trousers and long-sleeved shirts. Check your skin for ticks and should you find one remove it as soon as possible. Simple tools for this are widely available and the best way to ensure complete removal.

You are likely to encounter cattle when walking on the moor and whilst incidents are rare, there have been cases of ramblers being trampled on Dartmoor. Advice is to move quickly and quietly and if possible walk around the herd. Avoid getting between cows and their calves. Keep dogs on a short lead but if threatened let it go as cattle will chase the dog not you. If followed don't panic as most cows will stop before they reach you. If you feel at risk from a herd find another route.

Some of the walks enter into military firing ranges and it is essential to check that these are not in use before setting off.

Some more general advice –

- Especially if walking alone or into the centre of the moor, tell someone where you are going and when you expect to return, but don't forget to tell them when you are back.
- Take plenty of food and drink – especially drink in hot weather.
- Don't try to walk further or faster than you, or any of your party, can easily manage.

Obviously the risks are greater on longer walks well into the moor and in fine weather the shorter walks on paths should present little difficulty, however always be watchful, especially for mist. If mist falls it's easy to get disorientated and head the wrong way, even if close to a road.

Illustrating that things can go wrong for even experienced Dartmoor walkers, perhaps I should mention a couple of mishaps which occurred whilst compiling the walks for this book. Crossing the Butter Brook I slipped, landing flat on my face in the stream with a cut nose and leg and broken thumb. Fortunately I was close to the edge of the moor and two kind ladies, Ella and Katie, came to my rescue, but it was a lesson to take more care. The other occasion was more serious and no one was around. Walking to Wild Tor, on the lower slopes of Kennon Hill I experienced chest pains. With no phone signal, after waiting for an hour hoping someone would pass by, I walked very slowly off the moor. My wife met me and after initial care from a doctor in Chagford, an ambulance took me to hospital in Exeter where a heart attack was confirmed and a stent fitted. I was very fortunate, not only to survive the experience but that I'm still able to walk good distances on the moors. I now carry a satellite beacon.

It should be noted that whilst reasonable care has been taken in the compilation of this book, neither the author nor the publisher can accept responsibility for any inaccuracies, or changes that may have occurred since publication, and that it is the responsibility of the walker to take adequate precautions to ensure their personal safety.

My Dartmoor

My father introduced me to Dartmoor at the age of six and our first walk was to the Quarryman's Hut (beehive hut) near Haytor.

INTRODUCTION

I remember being slightly scared when the mist came down and excited when our bus had to reverse to pass a coach on the road up from Bovey Tracey.

My parents came from Devon so throughout our childhood we stayed with grandparents near Torquay several times a year, and Dad always took us on the moor, often three walks of different length, one for each child. My sister used to see pixies but as her elder brother it was my duty to be sceptical.

My second walk was along the Glazebrook from Wrangaton. I remember being intrigued at finding the source of the river but also being sick on the bus. We didn't have a car so Dartmoor had to be reached by public transport and I became used to long walks along lanes to the moor.

An early walk was from Bridestowe station, not long before the railway beyond Okehampton closed in 1968. Our walk had to be curtailed because I didn't like the strong wind on Arms Tor and we walked back round the lanes to Lydford. We'd taken a little spirit stove but it was too windy on the moor, so I asked Dad if they allowed frying on Lydford station. I couldn't understand why he didn't think it was appropriate to cook our bacon on the platform. One early walk was up Diamond Lane in the snow to Corringdon Ball Tomb, which we called the Mutilated Cromlech. Another memorable walk was to the Island of Rocks, before Meldon Reservoir was constructed.

As I got older we walked further and aged ten I reached Cranmere Pool in the centre of Northern Dartmoor, this time from Okehampton station. After that too closed we always took buses to the moor, often from Plymouth to Dousland and nearby villages from where we explored much of Southern Dartmoor. The longest walk was crossing the moor from Yelverton to Buckfastleigh: 20 miles with the road sections at both ends.

Another notable achievement was reaching Fur Tor but again transport was difficult. It was before the days of bus de-regulation but the only service to Princetown was an independent bus from Tavistock run by a Mr Striplin. We alighted at Rundlestone but on a very hot day the walk took longer than Dad had expected and we missed the return bus. As we walked along the road to Tavistock, with no hope of getting a train back from Plymouth before midnight, he resorted to thumbing a lift and a kind couple gave us a ride.

So it was Dad who introduced me to Dartmoor. We still say 'food, drink, map, compass' as we leave the house, the check list he recited before setting out for a walk. I can't say that every walk was enjoyable in its entirety, especially with 'waterproof' clothing consisting of a plastic mac and sou'wester, but as soon as I took my wife (then to be) to Devon we went on the moors. We got soaked walking to Huntingdon Clapper but unlike Mum who told Dad she'd never go on the moor again after they missed the train at Shaugh Bridge, she wasn't put off and accompanied me on many walks. Mum relented about twenty years later! Once we had our two boys family walks were shorter and often needed the enticement of lunch at Dartmeet or the Police Station Café in Princetown. They enjoyed climbing on rocks, often at Combestone Tor, and liked the quarries at Haytor and Foggintor.

More latterly some of my walks were to check routes for my father's book **Walks on Dartmoor : Paths & Trackways**. A culmination his of more than sixty years exploring Dartmoor, this describes walks along tracks, some well known and others not documented elsewhere. It took me to places I'd never visited and back to many spots that we'd walked to in my childhood. Several of the walks in this book are based on routes which he documented but didn't have room to include in his.

My last few years of walking have mostly been working out the routes in this book, often to very familiar places, sometimes to features that I last went in my teens and occasionally discovering things I'd never seen before. There is so much to find on Dartmoor and few people have seen more than a fraction of the antiquities to be found here.

I've walked extensively on Britain's coast, visited forty three tidal islands, forty of our most remote railway stations, climbed hills and mountains, but it is Dartmoor where I feel most inspired. The sense of thrill, wonder and anticipation of passing through a gate onto the moor can perhaps best be compared with entering a great cathedral or sporting arena. No two walks are the same and one could follow the same route every day of the year but experience something different. The air, the remoteness, the solitude, the numerous antiquities and the beauty all add up to make Dartmoor, England's last wilderness, arguably the most wonderful place in the whole of the country.

Thank you to Emily Woodhouse (*https://travellinglines.com*), author of *All the Tors*, an excellent read, for her assistance.

Map Legend
A Walks – Black
B Walks – Red
C Walks – Blue

WALK 1

SOURTON TORS ICE WORKS
& RATTLEBROOK RAILWAY

WALK 1A : SOURTON TORS ICE WORKS, CIDER PRESS & STONE CIRCLE : 2½ MILES *

WALK 1B : CONTINUES TO RATTLEBROOK RAILWAY & BLEAK HOUSE : 7½ MILES ***

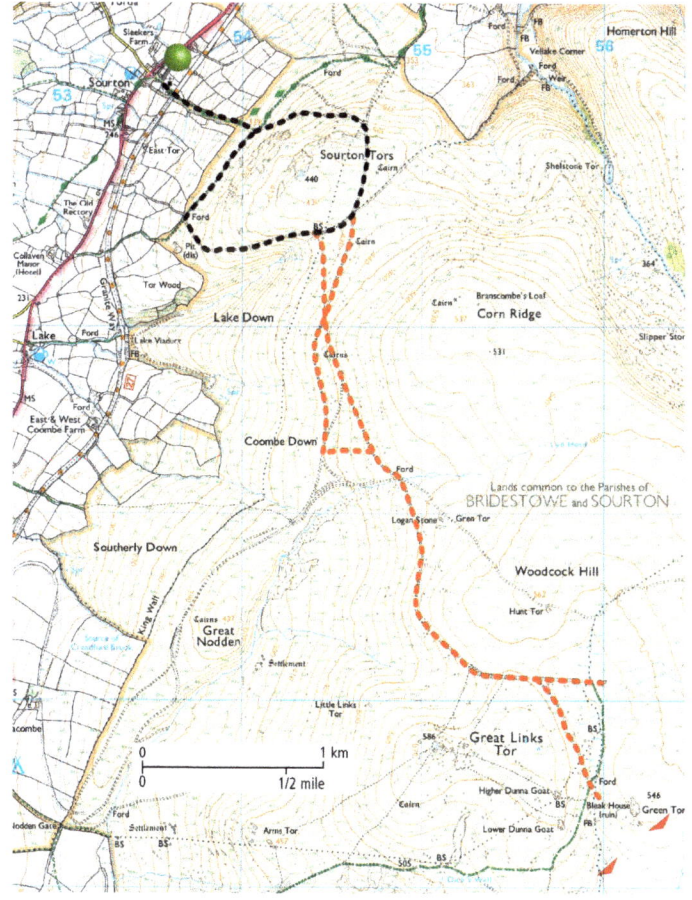

Walk 1A - An easy walk on paths, with one moderate climb, visiting one of Dartmoor's more unusual sites of industrial archaeology. The walk can be shortened to 1½ miles if the outward route is used back from the ice works.

Walk 1B continues along one of the moor's disused railways to the remains of Bleak House, once one of its most remote dwellings.

Start – Parking area by Sourton church (**535 903**).
Note that there is less space here on Sunday mornings,
or if there is an event at the village hall.

The tiny 14th century church of St Thomas à Becket nestles on the edge of the moor below Sourton Tors and holds services every week. The church is normally open and well worth looking inside. In the summer of 2018 it was closed to visitors for the unlikely reason that a pair of blue tits were raising their brood of eight chicks inside the lectern. To avoid disturbing them hymns were sung without the organ and after each service the birds received a blessing from the vicar.

Walk 1A

1. Follow the track to the right of the church which crosses over the old Southern Railway line (now the Granite Way cycle route), passes through a gate onto the moor and continues uphill between two walls (a strole). Stay by the left-hand wall. This is part of the **West Devon Way**, a 37 mile route from Okehampton to Plymouth.

2. When the wall bends left continue straight on along a track through a low cutting towards Sourton Tors. The track runs around the left side of the tors which are made up of many rocky outcrops, then divides just before some earth mounds.

Sourton Church

WALK 1

3. Take the right fork through the mounds, which are part of the remains of **Sourton Tors Ice Works** (*546 900*).

Sourton Tors Ice Works

During the 19th century there was a growing demand for ice to preserve food and prior to the development of mechanical refrigeration this was imported mostly from Norway. In 1875 James Henderson, an engineer, set up his ice works on the slopes of Sourton Tors, making use of Dartmoor's cold climate to harvest natural ice. The ice works consisted of terraces cut into the hillside, in which 32 small rectangular ponds were dug. These were fed by water brought by leats from a nearby spring. In winter ice from the ponds was collected and kept in an insulated stone storage building before being taken off the moor, mostly to be shipped by train to Plymouth for sale to fish traders. Unfortunately for Henderson, a combination of warm winters, losses from ice melting in transit and newly commercialised artificial refrigeration meant that his ice works was never profitable. His attempts to sell the business failed and it closed in 1886. Remains of terraces, ponds, an office and footings of the storage building can still be seen.

4. Join a wide track, the **King Way**, ~75 yards beyond the ice works and turn right. Two **marker stones** stand one each side of the track downhill to your left and another by the track on your right.

The marker stones indicate The King Way, an ancient track used by the King's Messengers to travel between Okehampton & Tavistock. It would have been a much easier route to ride than muddy lanes in the valley.

5. After ¼ mile a gulley by **Sourton Tors Sacred Pool** (*5459 8960*) is reached.

Whilst not everyone accepts that some of the many small shallow pools on Dartmoor were made by prehistoric people, the roughly circular shape and location on a saddle between hills and close to Bronze Age remains, suggest that this may well be a sacred pool.

6. ~20 yards to the left of the gulley is half of an **apple cider press** (*5462 8960*).

Carved from granite to crush apples for cider, this is one of a number of presses on and around the moor. It was probably abandoned after breaking in transit. The presses were operated by a horse pulling a stone wheel to crush apples as it rotated around the trough, which sloped inwards allowing the juice to be collected in the centre.

7. By the path to Corn Ridge, ~40 yards SE of the apple crusher, can be found **Sourton Tors Stone Circle** (*5466 8956*).

This is a large stone circle of 32 metres diameter. Most of the stones lie flat on the ground and the circle isn't obvious but it would be a most impressive monument were they to be raised.

8. Return to the pool. Walk 1B leaves here. For Walk 1A follow the right side of the gulley (a sunken track?), reaching a small **Boundary Stone** (*5447 8950*) after ~200 yards.

The stone is inscribed 'B' for Bridestowe on one side and 'SP' for Sourton Parish on the other. It is the starting point for the 'Beating of the Bounds' which takes place every 7 years.

9. Stay on the level track that bends away from the gulley, not a smaller path going uphill. Follow the track as it runs above a steep sided valley with a view to Lake Viaduct below, then bends around Sourton Tors, rising slightly as it goes beneath the spectacular rocks. (Alternatively follow a path by the wall.)

10. About half way along the tors take a grassy track diagonally left which leads down to the strole back to Sourton church.

Walk 1B

11. Follow Walk 1A to (8). Cross the gulley by the pool and continue straight on along the track (not any of the paths to its left that head directly up the hill). After ¾ mile this ends at an embankment (*5445 8838*). This is the **Rattlebrook Railway**.

Rattlebrook Railway

The Rattlebrook Railway was constructed in 1879 to link the peat works at Rattlebrook with the main line at Bridestowe. Built to standard gauge, for most of its life trucks were hauled by horses, but in the railway's latter days a petrol locomotive converted from a lorry worked the line. Its final job was to remove the rails when the railway closed in the 1930s. The cost of the line, which rose 1,000 feet over its 5 mile length, was a major factor in the peat works failing soon after they opened, although further attempts to run the enterprise took place over the next fifty years. In order to avoid the steep gradient of Corn Ridge the line was built with a reversing point where the trains doubled back and it is close to here that you join the route.

12. Cross the railway onto a grassy path initially heading diagonally left, which rejoins the line the other side of the reversing point after ~250 yards. Turn right and stay on the railway for 1¼ miles. The River Lydd is soon crossed on a **tube bridge** as it tumbles down the hillside and ahead is the mass of Great Links Tor.

13. Having climbed from the edge of the moor the railway descends through a cutting as it nears its terminus. The final section runs along an embankment before reaching the remains of the **Rattlebrook Peat Works** (*5596 8710*).

Bleak House

Peat cut from the surrounding moor was brought to the works where it was dried in kilns before shipping down the railway to Bridestowe. At its peak around 100 men worked here. The peat works were demolished by the army in 1961 at the request of farmers who feared for the safety of their animals and now just some low stone walls and rusting equipment remain.

14. After exploring the peat works return on the railway to the far (W) end of the embankment (*5563 8712*) from where a path runs to the left (SE). Follow this path for 0.4 miles towards the ruin of **Bleak House** (*5596 8648*) which soon comes into view. Just before the ruin head diagonally down to the Rattle Brook (there may be a vague path). Beneath the raised bank is a small pool and the brook can be crossed just above this. It can be very wet here.

Originally known as Donnagoat House, as it stood opposite the small Donna Goat Tors, Bleak House was perhaps thought to be a more appropriate name for this remote Dartmoor dwelling. Built from granite cut from the tor above, it was constructed to house the Rattlebrook Peat Works site manager. The house is now an atmospheric ruin with its chimney stack lying across the floor. Depressions on the slope above the house show areas where peat was removed.

15. Re-cross the stream (it is boggy on the Bleak House side) and return to the railway on the path.

16. Follow the railway again but continuing to the reversing point (*5455 8874*) from the very end of which (not the left) a path leads to the outward track. Cross the track and join the path around Sourton Tors, rejoining Walk 1A (8), close to the **B / SP Boundary Stone**. Follow Walk 1A back to Sourton church.

WALK 2

BLACK-A-TOR COPSE & BLACK TOR

WALK 2A : MELDON RESERVOIR, ISLAND OF ROCKS (OPTIONAL ****), BLACK-A-TOR COPSE : 4½ MILES **

WALK 2B : CONTINUES TO BLACK TOR : 5 / 7 MILES ***

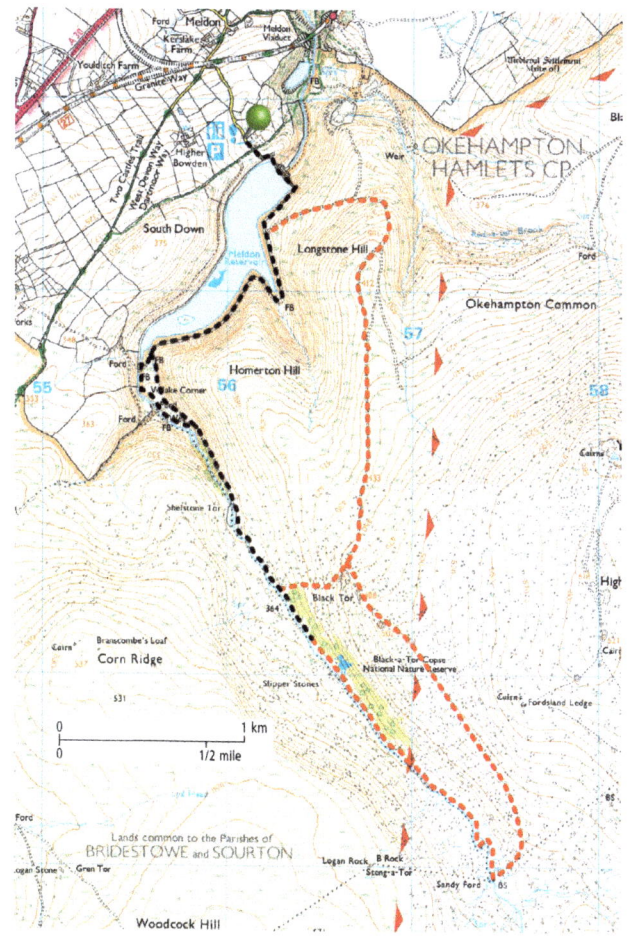

Walk 2A – A walk along narrow paths beside Meldon Reservoir, then along the pretty West Okement to one of Dartmoor's enchanted ancient woods. Optional diversion to the Island of Rocks, one of Dartmoor's hidden gems. Short section of rough walking beyond 2nd weir.

Walk 2B returns via Black Tor from where there are superb views in all directions. Steep climb and no paths to Black Tor.

Warnings:

Great care is needed should you decide to negotiate the rocky riverside to find the Island of Rocks. It is easiest to visit this in winter and spring before the vegetation grows.

Walk 2B - The second option for climbing Black Tor enters the Okehampton Firing Range. The first does not.

Start – Car park (charged) at Meldon Reservoir (**561 918**), just off the A30. Toilets.

Walk 2A

1. Ascend steps by the toilets and turn left onto a lane, reaching Meldon Dam after 125 yards. Cross the dam on the concrete walkway high above the gorge to one side and reservoir to the other.

The South West Lakes Trust tells us that 'Surrounded by steep sided banks and approximately 900 feet above sea level, Meldon Reservoir offers some of the most breathtaking scenery that Dartmoor has to offer'. To some this may be true but to others it is an intrusion onto the wild moorland that has flooded part of one of Dartmoor's most beautiful valleys. In 1962, just 11 years after Dartmoor gained the National Park status that many believed would protect it from such developments, the North Devon Water Board announced that its favoured location for a new reservoir was the West Okement valley at Meldon. The many objections were overruled and the last dam to be constructed on Dartmoor was completed in 1972. At 51 metres high and with a span of 201 metres, Meldon Dam is an impressive piece of engineering and to walk across it is quite an experience. There's no doubt that the reservoir set amongst moorland is highly picturesque but so was the gorge it flooded. The views downstream from the dam and those seen as you walk further up the valley illustrate the beauty of the moorland that was lost.

2. Turn right following a path above the water. Stay left of fence. Continue straight on where a path leaves to the left after 350 yards (this will be your route back for Walk 2B). The path narrows as it rounds an inlet fed by Fishcombe Water, a small stream running off Homerton Hill.

Towards the head of the reservoir is an island, which was formed as a nature reserve from spoil when Meldon was constructed. The original course of the West Okement was to the south of the island. When I did this walk in the very dry summer of 2018 the water was so low that people had walked onto the island and written their names with stones on the dried mud.

3. Cross the stream on **Fishcombe Bridge**, a wooden footbridge, and turn right, following the path as it runs above the water then descends to a grassy plateau at the head of the reservoir. It is possible to continue straight on to an arched stone bridge over the West Okement then follow the river bank, but this can be miry, so in wet conditions the easier option is to stay on the track to the left of the plateau. Either way reaches a weir & narrow bridge at **Vellake Corner** after ~¼ mile. Don't cross the bridge.

4. To reach the **Island of Rocks** (*558 903*) walk up the (left) river bank from the weir. There is no path, the going is rough with many rocks and in summer much bracken to negotiate. Great care is required. Hence this is only shown as an option in the walk.

The Okement tumbles over huge boulders as it descends through the trees in a series of cascades. ~200 yards upstream from the weir it splits, running either side of a narrow, 90 metre long rocky island. Writings and early 20th century postcards refer to the Island of Rocks and Rocky Valley, although neither name seem to be in regular use now and Valley of the Rocks is a more common name for this little-visited *glen. The valley has changed considerably with much tree growth since I first visited here in the late 1960s. Whilst following the river beyond here is possible and reveals some beautiful cascades, it is very rough walking and a difficult climb out at the top.*

5. Return to the weir, turn right and rejoin the track running along the steep embankment above the West Okement gorge, glimpsing the river below as it crashes spectacularly over boulders.
6. The track ends at a walled enclosure by another weir after ~0.4 miles. The next 150 yards can be boggy and requires picking your way through rocks, so less able walkers may wish to turn back here.
7. Follow the outer wall of the enclosure (there isn't much of a path here) until regaining the river bank after ~150 yards, where a good path is joined. You are now on open moor and it is a most picturesque walk for ⅓ mile to **Black-a-Tor Copse**.

One of High Dartmoor's three ancient high-altitude woods (Piles Copse & Wistman's Wood are the others), Black-a-Tor Copse is a National Nature Reserve. With oaks twisted and stunted by Dartmoor's winds and granite boulders covered in moss & lichens, it is truly an enchanted place. To protect the fragile habitat please do not enter the wood and avoid stepping on moss-covered boulders.

At 380 metres above sea level it is the highest wood on Dartmoor and nationally important for the lichens and mosses which thrive in the damp, clean air. Black-a-Tor Copse is the only significant location in Britain for the very rare lichen bryoria smithii. Much of Dartmoor was once covered in such woodland but most was cleared in Bronze Age times. Black-a-Tor Copse survives because saplings grow between the dense clitter, protected from sheep that would

West Okement

Black-a-Tor Copse

soon eat them on open moor. To further protect the wood and prevent the more adventurous sheep from nibbling seedlings, in 2008 small areas of the wood were fenced off. With the copse lying two miles from the nearest road getting materials here was quite a task and a military helicopter was used to help transport 100 wooden fence posts and 300 metres of plastic netting.

8. With some climbing over boulders and ducking under trees a path can be followed along the river bank to the end of the copse. Rising from the opposite bank are the steep slopes of Corn Ridge and the **Slipper Stones**.

Smoothed by ice, the flat rocks on the side of the valley known as the Slipper Stones are more typical of mountainous areas. They have a sad place in history as in December 1943 a US Liberator aircraft crashed here with the loss of ten lives while on an anti-shipping operation.

9. Walk 2B continues to Black Tor high above, but if you wish to avoid this steep climb Walk 2A returns on the outward route along the valley.

Black Tor

Walk 2B

10. Follow Walk 2A to (9). There are two options for the climb to Black Tor on the hillside above. The first is the shortest but steepest. The second adds ~2 miles to the route but with more wonderful river walking, a superb view and is slightly less steep.
11. The first option is to walk back down the river from the copse for ~100 yards, then follow a vague path on the right (E), which leads towards the base of the largest rocky outcrop. Take care as there is much clitter beneath the tor. Faced with an almost shear face it is easiest to make your way around the left side to reach the easily climbed north side of the tor.
12. The second option is to follow the river beyond the far end of Black-a-Tor Copse but cannot be taken if there is live firing in Okehampton Range. Continue by the river, passing the range marker pole, then reaching **Sandy Ford** (*5741 8793*), a crossing place over the Okement, after ~200 yards (just before the valley widens). A small **Boundary Stone** inscribed 'OP' can be seen close to the ford.
13. Do not cross the Okement but ascend the hill (left) following patchy narrow paths rising from the river. There is a wonderful view up the valley into central Dartmoor. Bear left (NW) as the

hill becomes less steep (not straight on to Fordsland Ledge) and **Black Tor** will soon come into view.

It is worth the effort to climb Black Tor as the views in all directions are superb. Looking off the moor a huge expanse of North Devon can be seen, while to the east is High Willhays, the highest point on Dartmoor. The best views of the moor are from the smaller (but higher outcrop) furthest from the reservoir. From here the West Okement makes a breathtaking sight as its valley heads into the moor. Beyond Amicombe Hill to the south is Fur Tor and the centre of Dartmoor's northern wilderness. Half a mile to the south east a military hut can be seen at the top of the hill. This is Fordsland Ledge, one of my favourite Dartmoor viewpoints. The walk could be extended here, but there is no path and it is quite boggy.

14. To commence the return route head N from the most northerly part of Black Tor (closest to Meldon), heading for a track which can be seen running across the hillside ahead. Aim for three granite blocks by a small stream (may be dry) 200 yards ahead (**5670 8971**), which mark the start of the track.

15. Initially stony, then grassy, the track is an easy route along the ridge to the Longstone Hill, where it passes close to the summit, a military **flagpole** and somewhat ruined prehistoric **cairn**. To the right is the picturesque Red-a-ven valley (Walk 3), with West Mill Tor and Row Tor beyond.

16. The track bends sharply to the left and descends quite steeply towards the reservoir.

To the right can be seen Meldon Viaduct, which once carried express trains from London to Plymouth. Built from iron in 1874, it is one of only two remaining viaducts in Britain to use iron lattice piers to support cast iron trusses. Sadly the railway beyond Okehampton closed in 1968, although the viaduct continued to be used for shunting operations by Meldon Quarry until 1990 when it was deemed unsafe to carry rail traffic. It remains in use for The Granite Way, a cycle and footpath between Okehampton & Lydford.

17. On reaching the reservoir and your outward path, turn right to the dam then cross this back to the car park.

WALK 3

BLACK DOWN MILITARY TARGET RAILWAY, RED-A-VEN DIP & VALLEY

WALK 3A : FITZ'S WELL, BLACK DOWN MILITARY TARGET RAILWAY & RED-A-VEN DIP : 3 / 5½ MILES *

WALK 3B : CONTINUES TO RED-A-VEN VALLEY & MELDON MINE : 4 / 6½ MILES **

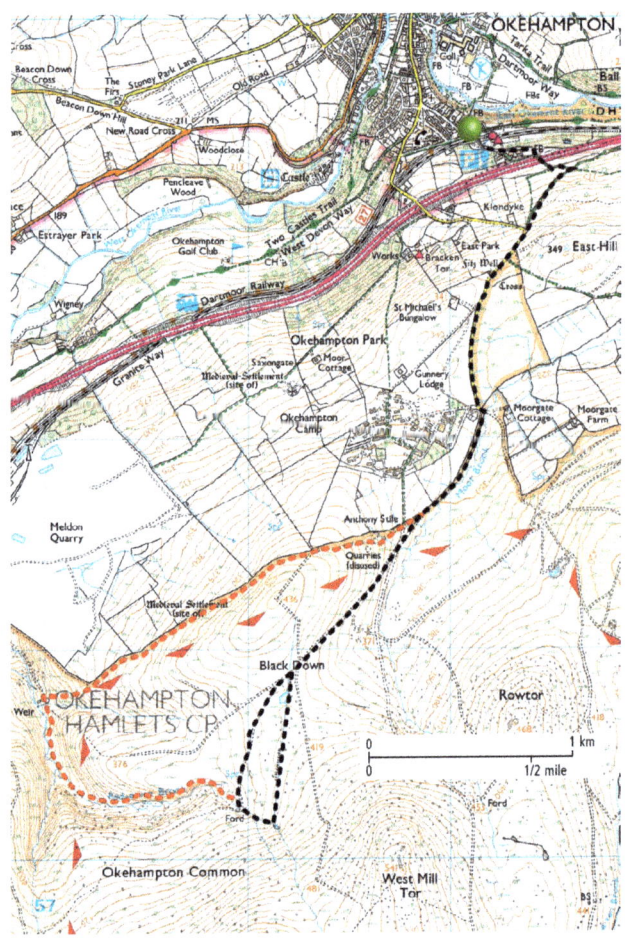

WALK 3

Walk 3A - An easy walk on good paths, with some moderate climbs, from Okehampton station to the tiny Red-a-ven Dip reservoir. The walk can be shortened to 3 miles by parking at Okehampton military camp (start the walk from 6).

Walk 3B continues into the picturesque Red-a-ven valley, passing Meldon Mine and enjoys panoramic views returning along the north side of Black Down. The walk can be shortened to 4½ miles by parking at Okehampton Army Camp (start from 6).

Warnings:

Most of both walks are within the Okehampton firing range.

Walk 3B - Care required on narrow path on the steep bank of Red-a-ven gorge.

Start – Okehampton railway station (**592 944**).
There is parking at Okehampton station (south side) designated for Dartmoor walkers.

Red-a-ven Valley

For the shorter options, small parking area on road adjacent to Okehampton Camp, immediately before the cattle grid to the moor (**5913 9316**).

Walk 3A

1. If arriving by train cross the footbridge to the car park for Dartmoor access (opposite side to the town). Turn left up the lane.
2. After 100 yards (just before some houses) follow a 'Permitted Route to Dartmoor' sign through a gate on the left. Follow the path into **Station Wood**, taking the right fork when it divides after ~60 yards. The wood was once part of Okehampton Castle deer park and contains a small reservoir which was used to provide water for steam locomotives.
3. After ~200 yards take a path right, again signed 'Permitted Route to Dartmoor'. This runs uphill to a high footbridge over the A30. Cross the bridge and take the footpath heading left, which soon bears right towards a gate.
4. Pass through the gate and turn right, following a path alongside the wall on the slopes of East Hill. In early summer the hillside is a mass of bluebells.
5. On reaching the road turn left. After ~300 yards, just before the road bends left, **Fitz's Well & Cross** (**5919 9379**) can be seen on the right.

East Hill

A natural spring, Fitz's Well was enclosed with granite slabs in the 16th century by Sir John Fitz, who owned land around Okehampton. A cross was erected, possibly having been moved here from St Michael's Chapel at nearby Halstock, which had been destroyed during the reformation. It stands

Black Down Target Railway looking to Yes Tor

quite low by the well but may have lost some height in restoration. The well still flows, although is now covered for safety reasons.

As would be expected, Fitz's Well has its own legend and it is said that a girl drinking from it on Easter Day will be married within a year. This originates from a couple who became lost when pixies brought down mist on the moor. They knew that to drink from a clear spring would break their spell and on finding what was to become Fitz's Well quickly drank some of its fresh water. Immediately the mist lifted and they could see their way home to Okehampton. The grateful man erected a cross by the well, the waters of which were deemed to hold the magical properties to determine a young lady's future.

6. Follow the road for a further 0.4 miles until it reaches the entrance to Okehampton Camp. Cross the cattle grid by the Range Warden Hut and take the right fork on a military road which runs beside the Moor Brook.

7. After ½ mile the road passes through a metal gate then bends left to run between Rowtor and West Mill Tor. This is the way for the popular route to Yes Tor (Dartmoor's highest named tor) and High Willhays (the highest point in Southern England). Don't follow the road but continue straight on along a stony track. You are now in the Okehampton Range.

8. Follow the gently rising track with West Mill Tor and Yes Tor to the left. After ½ mile, almost at the top of the hill, ~50 yards before a distinctive grassy mound (left), a low straight bank crosses the track. This is the **Black Down Military Target Railway** (*5820 9187*). It runs directly in a line towards Yes Tor and is marked as a waterway on the OS Explorer map.

The military built a number of short railway lines of various types to facilitate training with moving targets. The 960 metre straight north – south alignment on Black Down was constructed in the late 19th century and its earthworks are well preserved. The earthworks of another later curved target railway can also be seen. The railways operated on a pulley system, with men-shaped silhouette targets on sledges hauled by stationary engines or horses. They closed around 1960 and finds of 0.5 solid rounds suggest use for training with Boys anti-tank rifles, which were employed by the British Army in WW2.

9. Follow the railway, which heads directly towards Yes Tor and soon passes a pond on the right. Some metal **relics of the track** can be seen in the ground just before the pond. After ~¼ mile it changes from a bank to a channel which once held a pipe

Red-a-ven Dip

taking water from the Red-a-ven Brook. Soon after this, on the left by a path that crosses the track, is a low **marker stone**. This is inscribed 'NDWB' denoting North Devon Water Board. Beyond this a **drain cover** marked 'Willey & Co. Ltd SAV Exeter'.

10. After a further ~¼ mile the track ends a few yards before **Red-a-ven Dip** (*5183 9115*).

A small pool formed by damming the infant Red-a-ven Brook as it descends the valley between Yes Tor and West Mill Tor, Red-a-ven Dip was once a reservoir for Okehampton Corporation Water Works. At only about ten yards square the pool cannot have acted as more than a small supplement to the town's supply and may have been little more than an extraction point, but it is marked on the 1940 OS map as a reservoir. Water was taken through a pipe running along the course of the railway to a filtration plant at Anthony Stile on the Okehampton Camp boundary. With a lone hawthorn tree standing above it and water cascading over rocks, the tiny pool is a most attractive Dartmoor feature. The unusual name for the brook comes from the red veins found in the stream.

11. The small dam can be crossed with great care if you wish but then return to the original side and walk back ~30 yards to where a grassy path descends on the right side of the stream.

12. After ~200 yards this meets a track just above a ford. Turn right onto the track.

13. For Walk 3A stay on the track as it ascends Black Down, reaching the point where you left it for the railway after ~0.4 miles. Follow the outward route back to the start. You may however first wish to make a short diversion following the railway northwards for ~300 yards to its terminus in a cutting. The two static engine sheds once stood here.

Walk 3B

14. Follow Walk 3A to (12). Turn right following the track for ~100 yards until it reaches a green grassy area (may be boggy) just beyond a small stream (may be dry) which feeds into the Red-a-ven. Turn left across the green area and after ~50 yards pick up a vague path right which runs initially downhill around a dip in the land.

15. The valley narrows as the stream bends sharp left. A narrow path can be seen on the steep bank ahead. Aim for this and follow the path downstream with care as it is quite precipitous in places.
16. The brook runs through the steep sided valley which then opens out into an attractive grassy area with mountain ash trees by the water.
17. After ~½ mile of delightful walking a small stream comes in on the left through a valley beside Longstone Hill. Soon after the confluence the valley narrows again. Stay on the path by the river, walking towards a fenced gorse–covered mound (right of path) which is part of **Meldon Mine** (also known as Devon Copper Mine and Okehampton Wheel Maria)(**5700 9176**). The Mether Brook is crossed just before the mine and another shaft is fenced off to the left of the path.

*Meldon Mine was originally prospected for tin but found to contain worthwhile deposits of copper. It was last worked in the 1920s. The mounds behind the fences are spoil tips around the engine shaft. A rubble-filled wheel pit (**5696 9174**) can be seen immediately below the shaft on the left, however this can be largely obscured by vegetation.*

18. Immediately after the mine turn right onto a grassy path ascending the hill. Meldon Viaduct can be seen to the left. On reaching the corner of a wall after ~250 yards (**5722 9184**) continue straight on (NE) along a path beside the wall, which is followed for ~1 mile. There is a good view of Yes Tor, then a superb panorama over North Devon & Cornwall and finally of Okehampton Camp.
19. Shortly before meeting the military road divert around an old quarry (the footings of buildings can be seen). Just beyond this a **boundary stone** inscribed 'L' can be seen by the dry stone wall. It is one of five in the area and L denotes 'Lydford'.
20. On rejoining the military road followed on the outward route turn left, arriving back at the parking place by the camp after ~0.4 miles. For Okehampton station follow the outward route from the camp, via East Hill, reaching the station after a further 1¼ miles.

WALK 4

BELSTONE, CULLEVER STEPS POOL, IRISHMAN'S WALL, NINE MAIDENS : 3½ MILES *

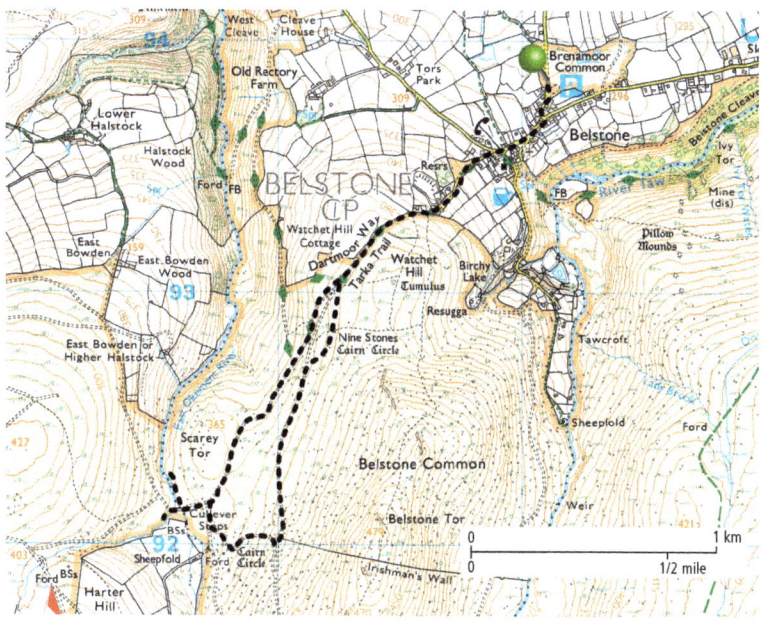

An easy walk on good paths through the interesting village of Belstone, to a most attractive pool on the East Okement river, returning past Bronze Age remains.

Start – Belstone car park (**6212 9380**) on the edge of the village approaching on the lane from Tongue End Cross & the A30.

1. Turn left from the car park, following the lane through the village. *The charming village of Belstone is an excellent gateway to the moor but it is well worth pausing to view some of its interesting buildings and antiquities. To the left on entering the village centre are the stocks which are thought to have been last used in the mid-1800s. They were restored in 1953 as part of the coronation celebrations and the granite seat added (an upturned pig trough).*

Just beyond these is Belstone Manor Pound, where stray or illegally pastured livestock would be held until payment of the appropriate fine. The last poundkeeper was a William Brock, who once suffered the ignominy of having his own cow brought to him by the local police constable and having to pay 5 shillings to the Lord of the Manor. The pound fell into disuse after Brock died in 1913 and for some time was used as the village dump, but in 1988 was converted to a walled garden for quiet contemplation.

To the left of the village green is the Methodist Chapel, which dates from 1891 but now only holds occasional services. The schoolroom added in 1926 is used as a tearoom and makes an excellent place to enjoy refreshment after a walk on the moors (open afternoons Friday – Monday). A memorial stone on the green was erected to commemorate the coronation of George V and later inscribed to mark the Silver Jubilee of Queen Elizabeth II. Beyond the green is the Tors Inn and behind it St Mary's Church, of Norman origin but largely rebuilt in the 19th century.

2. Follow the lane on the right of the village green then take the left fork (no through road) just after the Zion Chapel, which was built by non-conformists in 1841 and later served as a Post Office from which the Telegraph Office sign remains.
3. Follow the road as it climbs up to the moor, passing Belstone Water Works. Pass through a gate after ¼ mile and turn right onto a stony track running beside the wall. This is the track to Knack Mine, a tin mine on the slopes of Steeperton Tor.
4. Stay on the stony track, ignoring paths to the left, walking left of Scarey Tor and descending to the East Okement River at Cullever Steps (right fork at a triangle of paths just above the river).

Stepping stones are no longer obvious but there are bridges over the East Okement &

Boundary Stones

Black-a-ven Brook, which joins it a few yards downstream. To the left of the first bridge are the abutments of another bridge which was never completed. Apparently the military asked local people to build two bridges and rather than one across each stream they started to construct two next to each other over the Okement. Adjacent to the bridges are fords with paved beds, which were put down by the military in the 19th century so that horse drawn gun carriages could cross.

5. Cross both bridges to visit a **boundary stone** on the far side of the Black-a-ven.

This is marked as 'BSs' on OS maps as there are actually two boundary stones. The large stone inscribed 'OPB' denoting 'Okehampton Parish Boundary' is the most recent and the smaller stone beside it the original.

6. Re-cross the bridges and take a grassy path immediately on the left, heading downstream close to the Okement, then the 2nd branch left after ~30 yards (downhill) reaching **Cullever Steps Pool** (**6055 9225**) after ~100 yards. The first branch left also goes to the pool but tends to be wet.

The small pool, known as Cullever Steps although actually a little downstream of these, is a popular wild swimming spot. Set in a natural amphitheatre, surrounded by rocks one side and a grassy bank on the other, it is a beautiful

Cullever Steps Pool

spot to sit for a while even if you don't fancy a dip. The natural pool was enlarged by a dam which was built to deepen it for swimming.

7. After enjoying the pool return to the track by the bridge. Turn left, retracing your outward steps, then right where it divides at the triangle after ~75 yards.
8. After a few yards take the left fork, a stony track ascending slightly (not the right track running parallel with the river). A **marker stone** is passed on the left of the track.

Inscribed 'WD', this is a War Department range boundary stone, one of three in the Cullever Steps area. These and eight similar stones in the Okehampton area mark the boundary of the area leased to the War Department for military use in 1892.

9. Just before the track bends sharp left there is a **cairn circle (6078 9195)** ~35 yards to the right of the track.

Also known as a ring cairn, this Bronze Age burial site consists of a retaining circle, around a third of which is missing, surrounding a mound. A large flat slab propped against the outside of the mound may have been the cover for a cist. A flint knife dating from Early Bronze Age was found here after being exposed by heavy rain.

10. After visiting the cairn circle follow the stony track as it bends sharp left, then right and ascends gently. As it bends further right another track is approached and reached by a short grassy path. Follow this path, crossing the track and continuing for a short distance until it meets a tumbledown wall ascending the hill. This is the **Irishman's Wall**.

The wall, which runs for around $^3/_4$ mile from close to the East Okement, was constructed in the early 19th century, however never served its intended purpose. It was built by Irishmen, apparently in bare feet, with the aim to enclose an area of moor. The people of Belstone & Okehampton were not prepared to allow the wall to affect their access for grazing but chose to bide their time. However, once it had been almost completed, men from the villages turned out in force one night and armed with poles pushed over enough sections of the wall as to render it useless. Realising that to effect repairs would have been futile, the Irishmen quickly left but the remains of their hard work can still be clearly seen on the hillside.

Nine Maidens

11. Return to the track and turn right heading N for ~½ mile. Just beyond the most northerly outcrop of Belstone Tor above, at the end of a section where the track has a rocky base, take a grassy path (**6112 9274**) heading 45° right (NE). A stone circle is soon seen ahead. This is the **Nine Maidens** (**6123 9283**).

The Nine Maidens is actually a cairn circle and consists of 16 or 17 stones. It is also known as the Seventeen Brothers. The circle, which once surrounded a burial cairn, is of Bronze Age origin, although legends suggest that it was formed by nine maidens who were turned to stone, either for dancing on a Sunday or for practising witchcraft. It is said that the stones can be seen dancing at noon each day.

12. From the Nine Maidens take a path due N (diagonally left from your approach), which climbs a little before reaching your outward track by the wall and returning to the moor gate after a further ~¼ mile. Follow the lane back into Belstone.

The walk can be extended by ¼ mile by walking NE from the car park across Brenamoor Common to an attractive pool where water lilies bloom in summer.

WALK 5

WILD TOR, WATERN COOMBE & WATERN TOR

WALK 5 : BUTTERN HILL STONE CIRCLE, WILD TOR, WATERN COMBE, WATERN TOR : 7½ MILES ***

WALK 5 : RETURNS BESIDE RIVER TEIGN : 6½ MILES ****

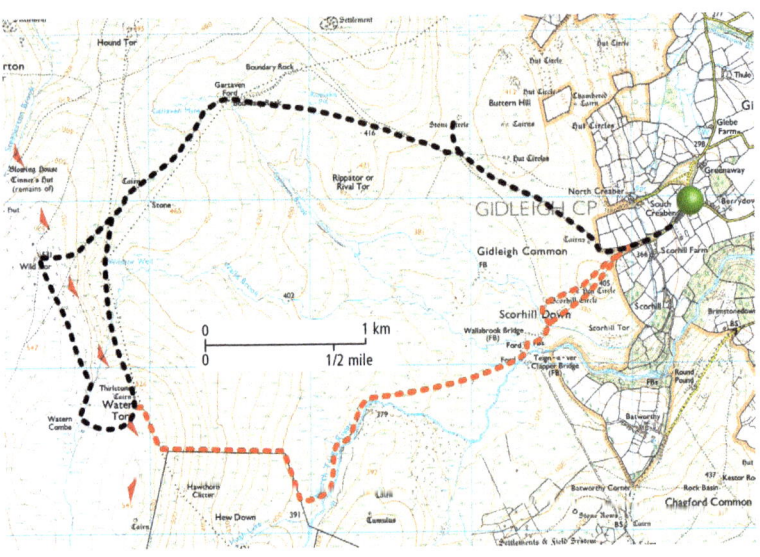

Walk 5A — A varied walk, mostly on paths but with potential for some boggy areas, visiting a remote tor with superb views, another with remarkable rock formations and a hidden gorge.

Walk 5B — Returns beside the River Teign passing through boggy areas.

There is limited parking at Scorhill Farm and it may be preferred to combine with Walk 6, starting from beneath Kestor Rock and adding 2 miles to the routes.

WALK 5

Warnings:

This is a boggy area of Dartmoor so easiest to walk after a spell of dry weather.

A small section of both routes is within the Okehampton firing range. This can be avoided by leaving out Wild Tor and Watern Coombe.

Walk 5B - The section along the North Teign is miry, particularly after wet weather. Be prepared to detour around bogs but only attempt this route if you are suitably attired and competent at such walking.

Start – Scorhill Farm (**6612 8774**). A small parking area reached on narrow lanes from Chagford (3 miles) passing through Murchington.

Walk 5A

1. From the car park pass through a gate into a strole which leads to Gidleigh Common & Scorhill Down. Take the path by the wall on the right.
2. At the end of the strole find a path which heads diagonally right (NW) from the wall, passing by two cairns. If you miss this path stay by the wall until it bends right after ~200 yards, then turn left onto a path from South Creaber.
3. Two wide grassy tracks can be seen on the edge of Buttern Hill ahead and either can be followed as they meet up at Sandy Ford (**6493 8827**) after ~½ mile. The ford crosses a small stream which is sometimes dry. A panorama of the whole walk can be seen from here. Wild Tor is ahead (slightly left). Looking back Kestor Rock can be seen on Chagford Common.
4. Just after the ford take a narrow path right, in the dip between the hills. After ~200 yards **Buttern Hill Stone Circle** (**6495 8848**) is seen ~40 yards right, on the lower slope of Buttern Hill. *Probably the least visited of the arc of stone circles in this corner of Dartmoor, Buttern Hill Stone Circle generally provides the visitor with solitude and fine views across the moor. Only 5 of the 23 stones are*

Buttern Hill Stone Circle

standing and some show marks indicating that they have been worked by stone cutters.

5. Return to the wider path at Sandy Ford which divides here. Take the left fork running WNW (not another path 90° left), gently ascending as it runs around the lower slopes of Kennon Hill.

6. After ⅔ mile this passes the bottom of a large tin mining gulley, **Ruelake Pit**, then crosses Rue Lake Ford, another stream that is often dry. Heading in the direction of Wild Tor, after ~⅓ mile this reaches **Gartaven Ford (*6348 8860*)** where the Gallaven Brook is crossed. On the south bank of the river is a large flat **boundary stone** inscribed 'GP', marking the limit of Gidleigh Parish.

7. Follow the ancient sunken track as it ascends from the ford, then bends left with Wild Tor ahead. Gallaven Mire is to the right, with the impressive Steeperton Tor beyond it (identified by a military hut close to its summit). The path may be patchy towards the top of the hill but keep heading towards Wild Tor (ignore a branch left). To the left of the path is **Wild Tor Well**, a dangerous area of mire. Keep clear of this.

8. Another path is met after ~½ mile from Gartaven Ford (***6291 8798***). Cross this and take a small path which starts to ascend **Wild Tor (*623 877*)**. The path soon peters out but the climb is not difficult. When the rocks go out of sight aim for a range marker pole below them.

WALK 5

From the extensive outcrops of Wild Tor there are wonderful views into Northern Dartmoor. Steeperton Tor is to the right (NNW), the high points of Yes Tor & High Willhays ahead (ENE) and Hangingstone Hill to the left (SSW). The distinctive Watern Tor is to the SE and Watern Coombe to the right of this.

9. To reach the Walla Brook and the bottom of Watern Coombe (SSE) either descend to the line of military poles and pick up a path (right), or follow a path to a lone fir tree then sheep paths to the stream.

10. Follow a path (right) beside the Walla Brook as it passes through **Watern Coombe** gorge (**627 870**).

A rarely visited but beautiful Dartmoor spot, the gorge of Watern Coombe emerges from the boggy area of the Coombe where the Walla Brook rises between Watern Tor and Hangingstone Hill. The stream rushes through the gorge, speeded by tinners' stone works that narrowed it to increase the flow and wash away their waste.

11. When the gorge widens into an area of tin workings a **tinners' hut** (**6262 8676**) can be seen. Cross the stream here and take a stony track which ascends diagonally left. Follow this (it soon becomes grassy) to **Watern Tor** (**629 867**).

One of Dartmoor's most distinctive tors, the remarkable rock formations on three outcrops of Watern Tor are unique on the moor. The tor appears to have been constructed by plates of granite being carefully piled upon each other to form heaps with strange shapes, but was actually formed in this way by cooling of the rock. From a distance there appears to be a huge hole through the rocks, however on approaching closer it can be seen that the two stacks are not joined. This feature is known as the Thirlstone and it is said that a horse could be ridden through the 'hole'.

12. Walk 5B leaves here, heading into the North Teign valley. For walk

Watern Tor

5A, which avoids the boggiest areas, take a path heading NNE from Watern Tor, returning to the Walla Brook at the lower end of Watern Coombe.
13. Cross the Walla Brook, and continue on the path which runs below Wild Tor, keeping to the left of a rocky area (**626 875**) below the tor in order to stay clear of Wild Tor Well.
14. Follow the outward route back ensuring you take the right fork towards Gartaven Ford where the path forks beyond Wild Tor (**9290 8798**).
15. If you wish to visit **Scorhill Circle** (**655 874**) (Walk 6) (extra ½ mile) take a smaller path just to the right of the main outward path at Sandy Ford, reaching the stone circle after ⅔ mile. A path left (E) then leads back to the starting point.

Walk 5B

16. Pick up a path which descends SE from the isolated outcrop at the south end of Watern Tor to the corner of a wall (**6311 8649**). The path runs roughly in the direction of a line from Wild Tor to the centre of the Fernworthy plantation ahead.
17. Follow a path to the left of the wall (don't cross the stile), staying close to the wall after it bends right, until just before it becomes a fence close to the North Teign. A path left from here cuts off the corner, missing out some boggy ground.
18. On reaching the river follow a path downstream. This is a picturesque stretch of river, although parts are boggy. Soon after the river bends sharp right take a path on the left which rejoins the river after ½ mile near **Teign-e-ver Clapper Bridge** (**6536 8707**).
19. You have now joined Walk 6 (see this for details of places of interest visited from here). Cross the **clapper** over the Walla Brook (the **tolmen stone** is in the river to the right) and take a wide grassy path diagonally left away from the river. This crosses **Gidleigh Leat** then divides.
20. To visit **Scorhill Circle** (visible ~150 yards away) take the left fork, or for the direct route back continue straight on over the hill. Scorhill Tor is visible on the right.

WALK 6

SCORHILL CIRCLE, TEIGN-E-VER CLAPPER, TOLMEN STONE & SHOVEL DOWN : 3 / 3½ MILES *

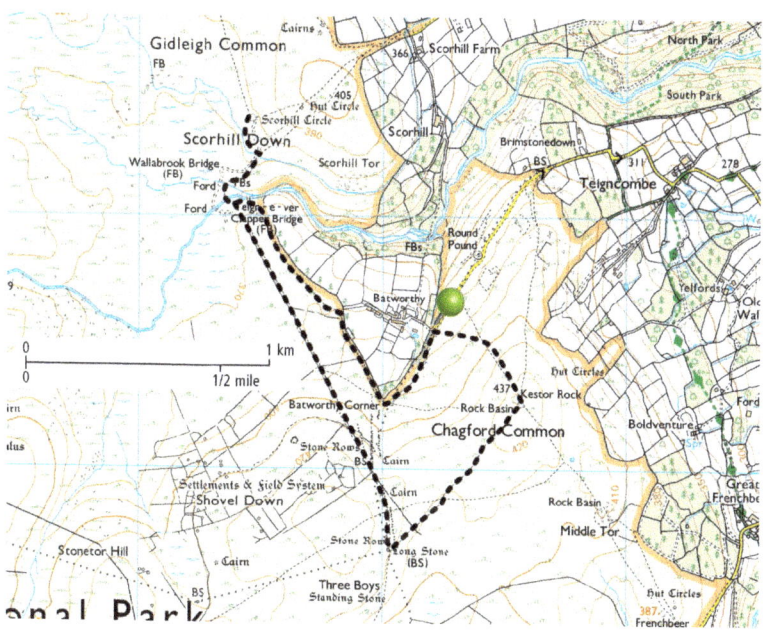

An easy walk on paths, visiting one of Dartmoor's most impressive Bronze Age stone circles, two clapper bridges, a remarkable rock with 'magical properties' and a splendid collection of prehistoric remains.

Start – Small parking area at Batworthy, adjacent to Batworthy Bridge (**6621 8657**) below Kestor Rock, at the end of the road through Teigncombe from Chagford. Additional parking is available in summer on the right before the end of the road.

1. Follow a rough track running parallel with the wall to Batworthy Corner (**6601 8628**).
2. At the corner turn right along a path running parallel to the wall,

Teign-e-ver Clapper

reaching the North Teign river close to its confluence with the Walla Brook after ⅔ mile. This attractive spot is a good place to stop for a while.

3. Walk upstream for a few yards, passing the remains of the original **Teign-e-ver Clapper** (*6545 8708*) and soon reaching the replacement **double span clapper** (*6536 8707*).
4. Cross the bridge and continue ~50 yards to the **Walla Brook Clapper**. Cross the single span bridge and follow a narrow path downstream for ~150 yards. Soon after it joins the North Teign is found the **tolmen stone** (*6551 8709*).

Dartmoor's tolmen is a large boulder lying in the river but close to the bank, with a hole through it formed by many centuries of abrasion erosion. With a diameter of around one metre the hole is large enough to climb through and of course has been said to possess mystical powers. Passing through the hole was claimed to cure children of rickets and to prevent rheumatism. The tolmen stone may have been used by Druids, who would have lowered a person into the water through the hole to purify them. Provided the river is not too high it is possible to climb through the tolmen but great care is needed. It is easier to slide down through the hole than it is to climb back but it would be a shame to cure the rheumatism and gain a broken leg in the process.

5. Return to the Walla Brook clapper and pick up a path heading slightly right (NW) reaching **Gidleigh Leat** after ~200 yards.

Constructed in the 16th century by tinners, the leat was diverted in 1653 by Bartholomew Gidley to provide water for his newly built Gidleigh Mill. It takes water from the Gallaven Brook and now serves just the farms at Scorhill, Creaber & Berrydown.

6. Cross the bridge over the leat and take the left fork, climbing gently to **Scorhill Circle** (***655 874***), which is reached after ~150 yards.

27 metres in diameter, with 23 stones standing and another 11 recumbent, Scorhill is possibly the most impressive of all Dartmoor's stone circles. It is thought to have originally had around 60 stones but some were robbed for repairing Gidleigh Leat and others show signs of being split by stone cutters. The tallest stone has a jagged point and if standing in the centre of the circle on midsummer's eve the sun can be seen to set over its tip, indicating that the circle may have had an astronomical purpose. It is one of 7 stone circles aligned in a curve around the edge of NE Dartmoor and with many Bronze Age remains on this part of the moor, may have been part of a larger ceremonial complex. It is said that horses are reluctant to pass through the circle, that it gives out natural energy and that it was home to a sheep-eating ogre. Whether the three legends are connected is unclear but the ogre may explain the horses' reluctance.

7. Return to the Walla Brook clapper, cross this then the Teign and take a path heading slightly right (S). This leads to a path running a little further from the wall than your outward route. It runs above Batworthy Corner and onto **Shovel Down** where there is an outstanding collection of Bronze Age remains.

Tolmen Stone

Walla Brook Clapper

The Shovel Down (or Shoveldon) remains include several stone rows all roughly aligned north to south, two standing stones, an unusual fourfold stone circle, cairns and ancient field systems. Although close to the popular Kestor, visitors are few and you are likely to have the hillside to yourself as you explore and contemplate the purpose of these ceremonial stones that have stood on the moor for 3,500 years.

8. The first of several **stone rows** is seen ~50 yards to the left of the path, level with Batworthy Corner. Stay on the path, soon reaching two **double stone rows** in a dip. The row on the left ends by the path at a **fourfold circle** (*6595 8602*), which consists of four concentric rings of stones, an unusual feature on Dartmoor. For the shorter option follow a path from here back to Batworthy Corner and along the track to your car.

9. Continue S from the fourfold circle, following a path along stone rows. The path from Kestor to Teignhead Farm is crossed and ~175 yards beyond this is the **Longstone** standing stone (*6603 8568*).

The 10 foot high Longstone, the fourth tallest menhir on Dartmoor, stands at the end of a stone row. Estimated to weigh around 4 tonnes,

WALK 6

it would not have been an easy task for the Bronze Age people to erect. It acts as a boundary stone for the parishes of Chagford & Gidleigh and Duchy of Cornwall land, bearing the inscriptions 'C', 'GP' & 'DC' on three faces. According to tradition the first man to reach the stone in the annual 'beating the bounds' would receive a prize.

10. Turn left (NW) at the Longstone following a path to **Kestor Rock** (½ mile).

The Longstone

The huge granite rocks of Kestor afford fine views across the moors. In 1856, a local antiquarian, Mr G.W. Omerod, discovered a rock basin on the top of the tor. It had been filled with stones and peat to keep sheep out, but when he excavated the hole it was found to be 2 feet 6 inches deep and eight feet wide – the largest rock basin on Dartmoor. According to legend, it was carved out by Druids for holding holy water and the blood of human sacrifices, but the less dramatic explanation is that these are formed by weathering of feldspar crystals in the granite. The rock basin used to be surrounded by a fence to keep sheep out and the holes for this can still be seen.

11. From Kestor Rocks take one of several paths downhill to your parking area. A **reave** (field boundary) dating from the Bronze Age (but possibly reused later), can be seen immediately beyond the tor and several **hut circles** stand on the hillside between the tor and road.

12. You may wish to visit **Roundy Pound**, on the far side of the road. *Probably built in the Bronze Age and part of the complex of settlements and reaves on the slopes of Kestor, excavation in 1952 found traces of iron ore suggesting that the pound was used in the Iron Age. It was also occupied in medieval times when low internal walls were added.*

WALK 7

FERNWORTHY RESERVOIR, MANGA & TEIGNHEAD FARMS

WALK 7A : FERNWORTHY CIRCUIT : 2½ MILES *

WALK 7B : FERNWORTHY, FROGGYMEAD STONE CIRCLE, TEIGNHEAD FARM, MANGA BROOK WATERFALL, MANGA FARM, STARKEY MEMORIAL, ROYAL MARINE MEMORIAL : 7 MILES **

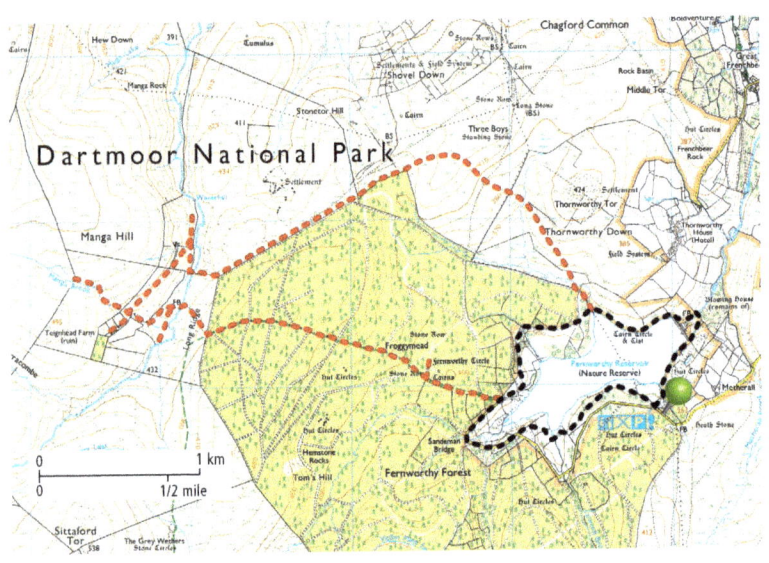

Walks 7A - An easy circuit of the picturesque Fernworthy Reservoir on a good path, passing a fine Bronze Age burial chamber. It provides a pleasant start & finish to Walk 7B which diverts through a forest onto open moor.

Walk 7B, also on paths but with potentially boggy areas, passes a Bronze Age stone circle, a fine clapper bridge, a hidden waterfall and the remains of a two remote Dartmoor farms, then returns past the memorial to a Royal Marine who tragically died on the moor.

Start – Fernworthy Reservoir car park. On right as the lane from Chagford meets the reservoir (**669 839**). Charged. Toilets. Refreshments March to end Oct Thurs – Sun, winter Fri – Sun.

Walk 7A

1. Take the path to the right of the toilets, staying on the stony track signed 'Round Reservoir Walk' and not walking to the water's edge. Turn right on reaching a track.

Completed in 1942, Fernworthy Reservoir holds up to 380 million gallons of water, supplying Torbay and Totnes. Surrounded by forest, it is a picturesque lake, especially in autumn. It's a popular spot to visit and a path can be followed around the reservoir, but also makes a good starting point for walks onto the open moor. When the water level is low a clapper bridge and hut circles are revealed on the bed of the reservoir.

2. After ~300 yards pass through a gate on the left and follow the path gently climbing away from the lake. After another gate this enters woods then crosses a footbridge, emerging into a picnic area.

3. Follow the path when it bends away from the lake, passing a bird hide. Go through a gate to short length of track which soon reaches the road. Turn right on the road. **Sandeman Bridge** is soon reached.

The bridge, which takes the forest road over the South Teign, was named after Edward Sandeman, the water engineer who designed Fernworthy dam. There is a nameplate on the left side of the bridge. Sandeman was apparently due to be knighted for his work on Derwent Reservoirs but after the news was leaked to the press King George V refused to attend the opening ceremony at Derwent Valley and the knighthood was never bestowed.

4. Continue slightly uphill on the road through the forest for a further ~300 yards until it ends at a clearing (**659 839**). Note a **gatepost** with slots. Walks 7B leaves here.

5. For Walk 7A pass through the gate onto a grassy path. At the end of the enclosure are two further gates. Go through the one on the right, following the path for ~50 yards to view the remains of an old farm building, part of the abandoned **Fernworthy Farm**.

The suffix 'worthy' was the Saxon word for an isolated settlement, suggesting that the Fernworthy settlement dated from before the Norman Conquest. A 1796 map shows a large house with buildings around it forming two yards. Fernworthy House, a sizeable two storey dwelling, was demolished when the reservoir was constructed and only this one stone ruin remains. It was attached to the house and had a slate roof but now just three walls stand, gradually being covered with vegetation.

6. Return to the gate and pass through the other gate. A further gate marks the entrance to an area of **Rhos pasture**.

Dartmoor possesses 20% of England's Rhos pasture, generally poorly drained acidic soil which is species-rich with grasses and rushes. This 5 hectare site supports a wide variety of fauna and is managed to promote devil's-bit scabiois, the host plant of the rare marsh fritillary butterfly.

7. The path passes through a gate into a wood. Note ancient walls and a gateway immediately on the left. A section of boardwalk crosses a boggy area before a footbridge over a stream.

8. Continue beside the reservoir, reaching **Thornworthy Cist** (**6675 8435**) just to the left of the path after ~275 yards.

The well preserved Thornworthy Cist retains all four sides and a large granite capstone leaning at an angle. A flint tool was found when it was excavated in 1879 by the antiquarian Samuel Slade and the founder of Torquay Museum William Pengelly. A smaller cist nearby was moved to the museum and can now be seen at the Dartmoor National Park Centre in Princetown.

9. The path continues beside the water to the dam. This cannot be crossed, so follow a gravel path which zig zags down to a footbridge and back up the other side. The car park is then reached after ¼ mile. A fine example of a Bronze Age **hut circle** can be seen on the left just after the dam.

Walk 7B

10. Follow Walk 7A to 4. Take the main track from the clearing heading uphill through the trees, then the left fork where this divides after ~150 yards. After ⅓ mile there is an opening on the right. In the centre of this is **Froggymead Stone Circle (6548**

Froggymead Stone Circle

8412). It is approached along the line of a **stone row**. To the right of the stone circle is a **cist** which was once beneath a cairn. These and other nearby remains are part of a Bronze Age ceremonial complex of which the stone circle forms the centre.

Comprising 27 upright stones, the same number recorded by Rev. Samuel Rowe in 1830, Froggymead Stone Circle is an impressive monument, although one feels has lost the moorland atmosphere shown in old photos prior to planting of the forest. It was excavated in 1898 when a trench was cut through the circle. No artefacts were discovered but beneath the peat were numerous pieces of charcoal, presumably from some kind of prehistoric ceremony or funeral pyre.

11. Return to the track and continue through the trees, going straight on at each junction, until coming out at a gate to the open moor (***6410 8433***) after just under a mile. Teignhead Farm can be seen ahead.

12. Take a path diagonally right (NW) leading to **Teignhead Clapper** (***6395 8450***) over the River Teign. This area can be boggy.

Teignhead Clapper was built in the early 19th century and provided access to the farm. It is said that the stones were transported from Manga Hill on sleds when the ground was covered in snow. With three parallel slabs it is unusually wide, having been constructed to allow a packhorse to cross.

13. Follow a path across **Manga Brook clapper bridge** and along the driveway to the remains of **Teignhead Farm** (*635 843*).

Teignhead Farm

Whilst it is often stated that Teignhead Farm was constructed in 1780, it did not appear in several surveys or maps produced between 1786 & 1804. Elizabeth Stanbrook's 'Dartmoor Forest Farms' documents her extensive research concluding that it was built by Messrs Crawford & Fleming and leased to tenant farmers from 1817. In 1897 the farm was sublet to a James Brock by the recently widowed Mrs Lamb. After a while Mrs Lamb decided that James was in need of a wife, so placed an advertisement for one. After meeting her at a railway station and conducting an interview, she decided that the lady was suitable for the position and introduced her to Mr Brock, who must have approved because he soon married her. They brought up two children in the farm and served teas to walkers to boost their income. It's said that Mrs Brock was not particularly house-proud, keeping a ferret in a kitchen drawer and allowing a pig to lie under the kitchen table as guests enjoyed refreshments.

The farm was inhabited until 1943 when it had to be vacated after military requisition, although in the 1960s it was lived in on an unofficial basis by a gentleman who spent his weekends here. He kept cats and would leave five days' worth of food for them when departing on a Monday morning. Teignhead was one of the moor's most remote farms, although the forest now makes it seem a little less isolated. After the roof fell in the house was demolished in 1971 but parts of the walls and a fireplace still stand. Three animal water troughs and various impressive gateposts are also of interest.

14. A tinners' **blowing house** containing an unusual **double mould stone** can be seen by the river (*6377 8428*). It can be found either by following a path along the N bank of the river from

Teignhead Clapper and continuing for a further ~100 yards after crossing the Manga Brook, or by following a raised bank from a kink in the wall E of the farmhouse.

The well-preserved blowing house is one of only seven on Dartmoor known to contain a furnace. The unusual mould stone containing two troughs into which molten tin would have been poured stands next to the furnace. A hollow adjacent to the northern wall is the remains of the wheel pit where a water wheel operated the bellows.

15. Return to the farmhouse side of Manga clapper bridge then climb the left bank of the stream as it cascades over rocks - **Manga Brook Waterfall**. There is barely a path but the little-visited waterfall is worth viewing.
16. Cross at the top of the falls where the stream splits just below a wall and pick up a vague path descending above the opposite bank to Manga Brook Clapper.
17. Turn left at the clapper following a path to Manga Farm. When this divides after a wall take the narrow right fork which leads to the farm driveway. Follow this to **Manga Farm** (*6391 8485*).

The thatched single storey Manga Farmhouse consisted of just three rooms. It was built around the same time as Teignhead Farm but was abandoned far sooner. A letter in 1884 to the Duchy of Cornwall from James Lamb, tenant of Teignhead, asks if he can use materials from the long-dilapidated farmhouse which had recently lost its roof in a storm, to repair an outbuilding.

18. Return along the impressive semi-paved driveway, which ends at a gateway where one of the **gateposts** retains its iron hangers. Turn left, walking beside the wall, then just before meeting another wall pick up a narrow path which descends to **Starkey's Clapper** (*6399 8463*).

This small clapper bridge was probably constructed by the owners of Manga Farm in order to shorten their route to Chagford. It was swept away when the Teign flooded in 1826 and lay on the riverbed until discovered by the Dartmoor writer F.H. (Harry) Starkey. After a public appeal for funds the bridge was restored in 1990. The bridge and an adjacent boulder with a small incised cross and an inscription (now hard to decipher) are both memorials to Harry Starkey who died in 1989.

Originally Manga Clapper it is now generally known as Starkey's Clapper.

19. Cross the clapper to view the memorial boulder then head diagonally left towards a gate and stile in the wall on the left, close to the forest. Use either to cross the wall then pick up a path heading alongside the plantation. Parts of this may be boggy. Kestor Rock can be seen ahead.
20. After ⅓ mile a gate into the forest is passed (**6476 8502**). ~100 yards beyond this, just to the left of the path is **The Marine's Stone** memorial.

Steven Perry was Regimental Sergeant Major of the Commando Training Centre at Lympstone. He sadly suffered a heart attack and died suddenly at this spot in 1992. The simple memorial is a large slab of granite, which originally stood upright but now lies flat on the moor. It was placed here by his friends and family. The crest of the Royal Marines is engraved on the stone above the inscription:

In memory of WO 1 (RSM) S.L. Perry RM
12.11.49 - 20.10.92

21. Continue on the path to a wall which is crossed on a stile, until reaching the corner of the (felled) plantation (**653 853**).
22. Take a path diagonally right (~ESE) which ascends the lower slopes of Shovel Down. This may peter out but there are a number of paths on the hillside and take any that lead to a gate (**6604 8521**) in the wall below Thornworthy Tor.
23. Pass through the gate then cross the Longstone Brook at a ford (**6609 8511**) by old mine workings. Continue on the path below the tor, reaching the flat rocks of Lower Thornworthy Tor (**663 848**) after 0.2 miles.
24. Continue on the path, then bear right towards a small clump of trees in a corner above the reservoir (⅓ mile SE of Lower Thornworthy Tor), where there is a stile & gate (**6671 8451**), then a take path leading straight on down to the water.
25. Turn left following the path beside the reservoir, passing **Thornworthy Cist** and below the dam (Walk 7A from 8), then back to the car park.

WALK 8

HURSTON RIDGE STONE ROW, BENNETT'S CROSS & VITIFER MINE : 3 / 3½ MILES **

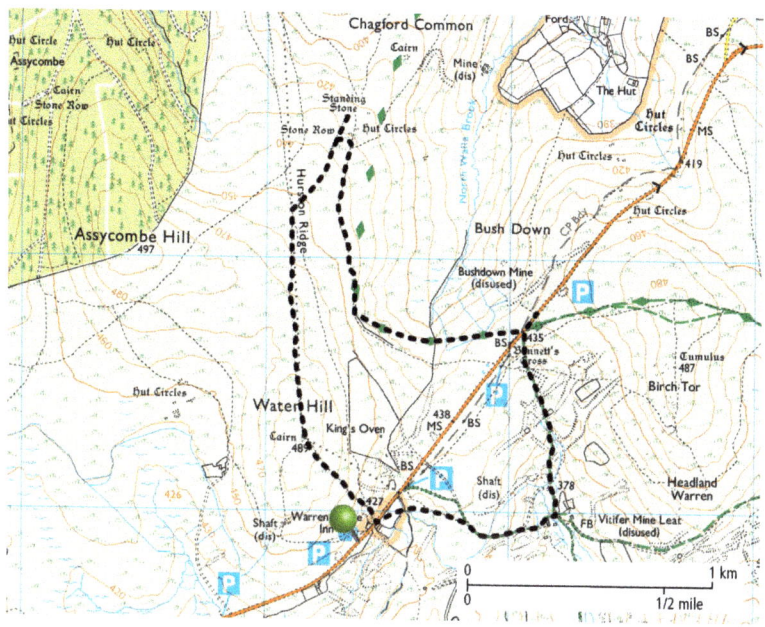

A walk on paths from Dartmoor's famous inn to one of its most impressive stone rows and the remains of one of the many tin mines in this area. Includes two climbs.

Warning:

Care should be taken around Vitifer Mine where there are many shafts.

Start – Warren House Inn (**673 809**) on B3212 Moretonhampstead to Princetown road. There are several small car parks beside the road.

43

The highest pub in Southern England, the Warren House Inn is also one of the most remote. It was built to serve tinners from the nearby mines but since the last commercial mine closed in 1930 has relied on passing trade and tourism. The current inn was built in 1845, replacing an earlier building on the opposite side of the road. Whatever the weather or time of year a fire can be found burning in the bar. It is said that this has been alight continuously since smouldering peat was brought across from the hearth of the original building in 1845. It now burns wood from local farms. The fire was originally kept alight to ensure that tinners would always have a warm refuge after a hard day's work and the tradition continued when the last mine closed. In the harsh winter of 1963 the inn was cut off by snowdrifts for 12 weeks and supplies had to be flown in by helicopter. The cosy pub with its fire makes an ideal stopping point for walkers on a cold day, or in summer when food can be enjoyed on the green opposite with superb views across the moor. Note the concrete lions which support four of the benches.

1. Take a path on the north (inn) side of the road at the end of the parking layby (~70 yards from the inn towards Moretonhampstead). This climbs Water Hill, passing workings from Water Hill Mine and reaching a **cairn** on the summit (***6716 8130***) after ~0.3 miles, from where there are excellent views in all directions.

The Bronze Age burial cairn has been altered over time, with stones robbed and others added more recently. During WW2 it was rebuilt as a crude lookout shelter with an iron roof added. For many years the cairn was referred to as King's Oven, however this is an enclosure nearby where tin smelting used to take place.

2. From the cairn take the path which runs N to the right of the plantation surrounding Fernworthy Reservoir, not the path heading left of the plantation or the smaller one on the right.

3. There are several paths on Hurston Ridge, some of which change over time, but none run directly to the stone row. The suggested route is to pick up a small path which branches to the right immediately before a short gulley, level with the start of the forest, ~¼ mile from the cairn.

WALK 8

4. Stay on the path, bending right across a green area, not forking left by some earth mounds and soon meeting a wider path. Turn left onto this and **Hurston Ridge Stone Row (6727 8244)** can soon be seen left of the path ~200 yards ahead.

Hurston Ridge Stone Row

One of Dartmoor's finest double rows, Hurston Ridge Stone Row runs for 150 yards and contains 99 stones arranged in 49 pairs. There is a blocking stone at one end and a small cairn at the other. The tall stone at the SW end is considered to be a menhir. A stone axe, urn and cremated bones were found when the cairn and row were excavated by the Dartmoor Exploration Committee in 1900.

5. After investigating the stone row walk uphill to its southern end, then turn 90 degrees left, returning to your outward grassy path after ~100 yards. Turn right onto the path (part of the **Two Moors Way**), which initially heads S gently ascending, then narrows and runs along the side of the hill, meeting a dry leat. Keep the leat on your left hand side, following the path beside it. As the leat disappears into the undergrowth, stay on the clear path that crosses a small stream (not the right fork) before climbing to the road at **Bennett's Cross** car park.

Bennett's Cross is one of a number along the road from Exeter to Tavistock. The 6 foot tall cross is quite unusual in having a kinked shaft and short arms. It is quite roughly cut and gives the appearance of having been made with minimum effort. The letters 'WB' are inscribed on the shaft, although are difficult to discern, probably denoting 'Warren Bounds', the extent of Headland Warren. It also marks the boundary between the parishes of Chagford & Bovey Tracey. Several explanations have been suggested for the origin of its name. Stannary records include mention of a 16th century tin miner with the name William Bennett and the cross may have marked the boundary of the area for which he had mining rights. The 'WB' inscription could have been his initials. A second suggestion is that Bennett comes from Benedict, for which it was a common corruption, and was named because it was on the road linking Benedictine monasteries at Exeter & Tavistock. A more recent possibility is from the late 1860s, when a gentleman by the name of Ellery Bennett apparently found the cross partially buried and had it cleaned then re-erected, so it was named after him.

6. Divert to visit the cross a few yards to the left (NE) of the car park, then 75 yards beyond a **Warren Bounds Stone.**

Inscribed 'WB', this small standing stone is one of 15 or 16 which marked the boundary of Headland Warren. The warren, which provided rabbits to feed miners, covered an area of 600 acres and ceased operating in 1920.

7. Take the path starting at a gap in the stones at the centre of the car park. (If preferred the walk can be shortened (3 miles, omits Vitifer Mine) by taking a path right after a few yards, which runs parallel to the road, returning to the Warren House Inn after ½

Vitifer Mine

mile). To the left as you leave the car park are two enclosures – **'The Aces Fields'**.

One enclosure is diamond shaped and the other roughly a heart. There are two different stories as to their origin but both involve a tin miner, Jan Reynolds. According to the first he lost all his money playing cards in the Warren House Inn and built the card-shaped enclosures as a reminder of the foolishness of gambling. In the other he dropped them when carried off by the devil after being caught playing cards during the sermon at Widecombe Church.

8. Follow the grassy path heading downhill, initially in the direction just right of Birch Tor. (Don't take another grassy path to the right heading towards trees, or the narrower path branching left to Birch Tor.) Several fenced-off shafts from **Vitifer Mine** are passed.

Vitifer Mine, along with Birch Tor Mine, which was owned by the same company, formed the largest complex of tin mines on Dartmoor. It extended down the valley linking with Golden Dagger Mine, and at its peak in the 1860s employed 150 people. Water came from a 7 mile leat running from the East Dart and ore was sent to Eylesbarrow Mine for smelting. Shafts were dug to up to 250 feet depth. Operations commenced around 1750 and underground mining ceased in 1913, although surface dumps were reworked until 1925. The extensive mining has had a considerable influence on the moor's appearance here.

9. Soon after crossing a small stream turn left on meeting a wider track ~0.4 miles from the car park. This once served Golden Dagger Mine, the last to close on Dartmoor. After ~150 yards extensive remains of Vitifer Mine (**682 810**) are reached by crossing a **clapper bridge** over the Redwater stream.

10. Walk through the remains of buildings on the right (these were once a **blacksmiths shop** and **miners' dry**) and take a path running uphill, passing a wooden **telegraph pole**, the only one remaining from the network that served the mines.

11. On reaching a wider track after ~125 yards turn left and follow this as it rises and bends right. The path forks after ~275 yards (**6784 8095**) and the Warren House Inn is now in view. Take the left fork which leads to the grassy area in front of the inn.

WALK 9

SHAPLEY TOR, HOOKNEY TOR & GRIMSPOUND : 4 MILES *

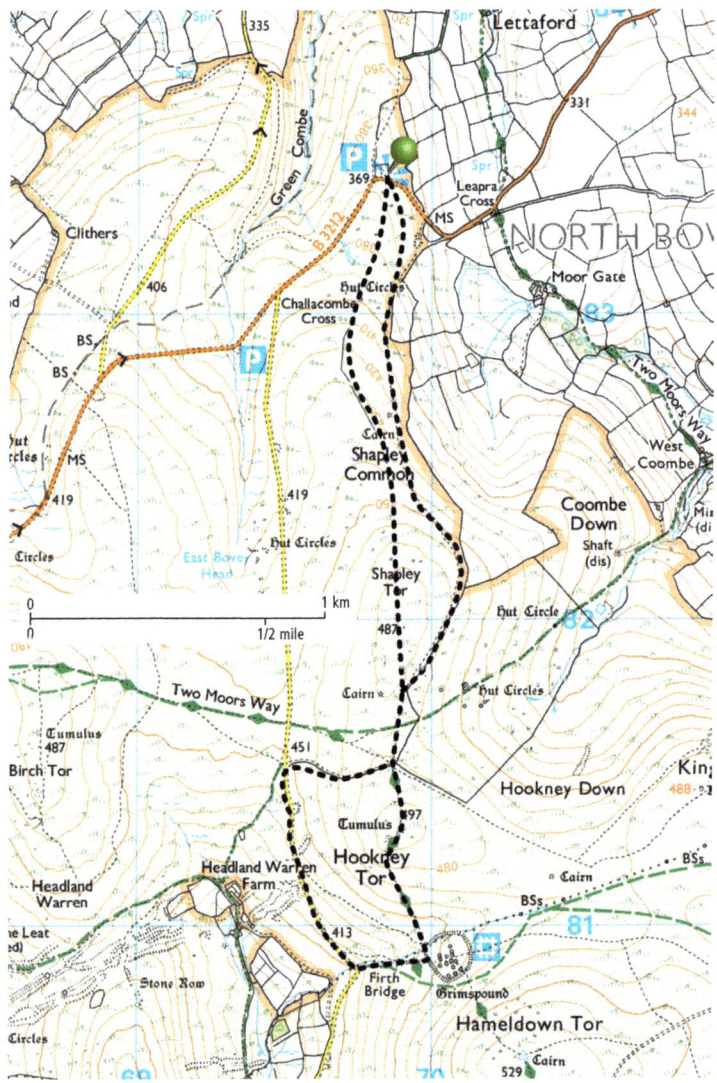

WALK 9

A walk on paths with steady inclines visiting prehistoric remains and two tors affording superb views. There is an excellent view from the car park but the panorama across the moor is exceeded from Shapley & Hookney Tors. The walk passes some fine Bronze Age hut circles and provides a spectacular approach to the best preserved prehistoric settlement on Dartmoor.

Start – Shapley Common car park on B3212 Moretonhampstead to Tavistock road (**698 834**). Ice cream van in summer.

1. Cross the road & take the path directly opposite the car park entrance, heading S onto Shapley Common. After ~¼ mile the path passes a small group of trees and several well-preserved **hut circles**. The first (**6977 8313**) is just before the trees and a further three ~75 yards beyond.

These excellent examples of hut circles were occupied by Bronze Age farming people around 3,500 years ago. The circles range from 5 – 9 metres in diameter and the most northerly lies within a small enclosure.

2. There are multiple paths on Shapley Common. Fork right ~125 yards after the final hut circle, reaching a **reave** (a prehistoric earth bank field boundary) after ~150 yards (or take any path which leads to the reave).
3. Turn left following the reave, then continue up the hill to **Shapley Tor**, a collection of rocky outcrops spread out near the summit of the hill.
4. Continue on the path from the furthest outcrop, descending to the corner of a wall, then turn right onto a wide path to a gap in the wall ~250 yards ahead (**6987 8152**).
5. Pass through this gateway and follow the path, part of the **Two Moors Way**, as it ascends to **Hookney Tor**, where there is a **tumulus** (**6990 8131**) and a good view of **Grimspound** ¼ mile ahead.

The tumulus, just E of the large granite outcrops of Hookney Tor, is a 20 metre diameter earth mound which was constructed in the Bronze Age as a burial cairn. It is one of the few of Dartmoor's cairns to have incorporated a natural rocky outcrop and includes a rubble bank on its south face.

Grimspound from Hookney Tor

6. Continue downhill to **Grimspound** (*701 809*).

The best-preserved prehistoric settlement on Dartmoor, Grimspound probably dates from the Late Bronze Age, 1450–700 bc. The remains of 24 hut circles (round houses) can be seen inside a 150 metre diameter wall. Averaging 3 metres thick and 1.5 metres high, the pound's stone walls are by far the strongest on Dartmoor, but its situation in a valley suggests that this was not for defensive purposes. Excavation in the late 19th century showed that they were actually two separate walls with a gap between them, and it seems that the purpose was to keep domesticated animals in and wild creatures out. The site was partially reconstructed after excavation but using modern assumptions as to how it originally looked. 13 of the 24 huts have been found to have signs of human occupation and the remainder were likely to have been for keeping animals. The Grim Lake, a tiny stream, runs through the north of the settlement and would have provided water. Grimspound is owned by English Heritage. Its name is relatively recent, and attributed to the Cornish clergyman & poet Rev. Richard Polwhele, who in 1797 was the first to record it. The name probably derives from Grim, the Anglo Saxon god of war.

7. Walk through the enclosure to the main entrance on the opposite (S) hillside. Here can be found **Grimspound Cross** (*7012 8085*).

This small cross, just 6 inches high, is inscribed into a large rock on the right hand side facing into the entrance. Little appears to be known about

WALK 9

it and it isn't mentioned in the main Dartmoor reference books. Its age seems unknown and some may consider it vandalism of a prehistoric remain.

Tinners' Hut

8. The return route is slightly less direct but goes around the hills. Take the path from the W entrance of Grimspound, descending to the road. A tiny **clapper bridge** is crossed after ~125 yards (**6983 8090**). This small single span granite bridge crosses a narrow stone-sided leat which takes runoff water to the Grim Lake. The leat is often dry.

9. The Grim Lake descends close to the path in a series of small cascades, reaching the road at **Firth Bridge**. Turn right along the lane, soon passing a **boundary stone** standing 20 yards left of the road.

Inscribed 'WB', this small standing stone is one of 15 or 16 that marked the boundary of Headland Warren, now Headland Warren Farm, which can be seen in the valley to the left. The warren, which provided rabbits to feed miners, covered an area of 600 acres and ceased operating in 1920.

10. ~¼ mile after Firth Bridge, just beyond **Headland Warren Farmhouse,** is a mining gulley on the right of the lane. Enter the gulley to visit a well-preserved **tinners' hut** (**6955 8123**) a few yards from the road.

11. Leave the road ~250 yards from the gulley, taking a path on the right, running left of a wall. The gateway which you passed through earlier en route to Hookney Tor is reached after ~¼ mile.

12. Follow the outward path for ~250 yards to the corner of the wall, then rather than climbing back over Hookney Tor stay on the path which runs close to the wall before bearing left to the car park.

WALK 10

WIND TOR & HUTHOLES : 1½ MILES *

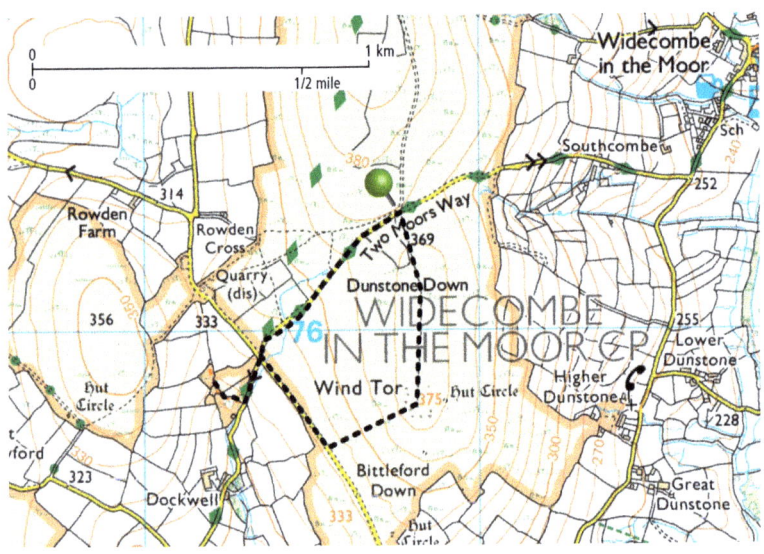

An easy walk on paths and quiet lanes, to one of Dartmoor's lesser known tors, with excellent views and some prehistoric remains, then to an abandoned 13th century village. One short steep climb.

Start – Two Crosses car park on Southcombe
road from Widecombe (**708 763**).

1. Cross the lane from the car park. The **Two Crosses Stone** and a **boundary stone** are seen beside the road.

This spot where a track crosses the road was once marked by two crosses cut in the grass and known as 'Two Crosses in the Turf'. The inscribed 'Two Crosses' stone was placed here in 2008. The boundary stone, which was erected in 1907, has no inscription but was positioned here to mark the boundary between the manors of Widecombe & Dunstone. Robert Dymond, who bought Dunstone Manor in 1869, had

WALK 10

Two Crosses Stone

planned to place either a double-headed cross or two separate crosses here, but died before this was carried out. A meeting of commoners in 1903 decided that the boundary stone should be erected.

2. Follow the path heading S up the gentle slope towards Wind Tor, which can be seen on the hill ahead. To the right is a **medieval enclosure** with earth walls. Shortly beyond this is another **boundary stone**.
3. ~100 yards from the end of the enclosure a number of rocks straddle the path. Immediately on the left of these is a half **millstone** (**7084 7601**), which was probably broken during manufacture and abandoned here.
4. Stay on the path as it climbs gently to **Wind Tor**.

Whilst not the largest of tors, the flat rocky outcrop of Wind Tor affords magnificent views across the moor. Notable landmarks are Buckland Beacon, Saddle Tor, Warren House Inn, Princetown and many tors around the East and West Dart valleys. There is a small shelter formed of an overhanging rock on the west side of the tor.

5. To visit a ruined Bronze Age **hut circle** (**7088 7580**) walk ~100 yards left (E) of the tor.
6. A **reave** (Bronze Age earth & stone field boundary) runs SW from the tor (the right side as you approached). Follow a path alongside this to the road below.
7. Turn right along the lane for 350 yards to a crossroads, then turn left. There is an old **gatepost** with the remains of hinges on the left at the start of the lane. After ~175 yards a finger signpost on

Hutholes

the right indicates a narrow path through a gate and into a small wood leading to Hutholes.

8. Follow the path, which allows public access but is not a designated public footpath. Please obey conditions on the notice, which include keeping dogs under close control, no picnicking & not climbing on monuments. **Hutholes (702 759)** is reached after ~150 yards.

The small deserted village named Hutholes is thought to have been the old manor of Dewdon which was recorded in the Domesday Book as Depdona. The ruins of six buildings date from the 13th century and were probably all that remain of a larger medieval village. The site was excavated in the 1960s by Mrs E.M. Minter and evidence found suggesting that earlier structures stood beneath the ruins. Several of the buildings clearly show the layout of Dartmoor longhouses, with dividing walls separating the area occupied by people and their animals. The village was abandoned in the 14th century, probably because of the worsening climate which meant it was no longer possible to successfully grow crops on Dartmoor.

9. Return to the lane and crossroads, then continue straight on, reaching Two Crosses car park after ⅓ mile.

WALK 11

HAYTOR QUARRY, GRANITE TRAMWAY & QUARRYMEN'S HUT : 2½ / 3¼ MILES *

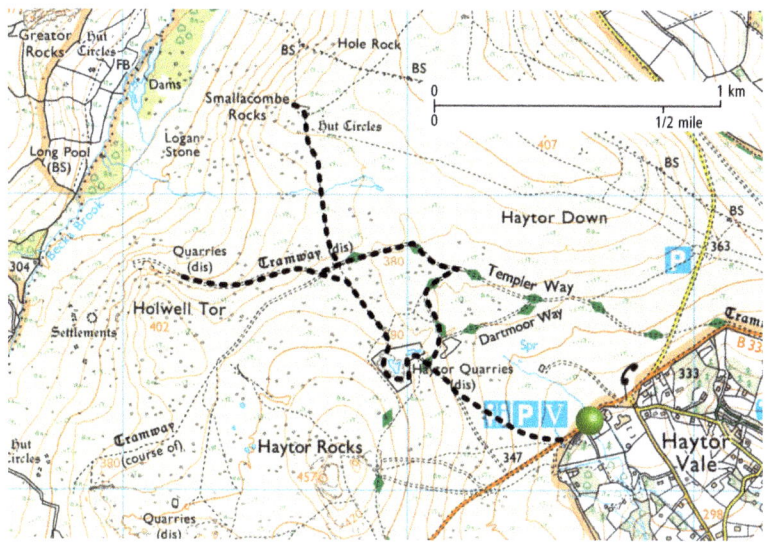

An easy walk on good paths to some lesser known historical features in the most visited part of Dartmoor. Not far from the main road, the immense rocks of Haytor attract more visitors than any other place on the moor. The majority however don't venture beyond the tor and few find the magical quarry, historic stone railway and hidden quarrymen's hut that are all easily reached in this short walk. Optional diversion to Smallacombe Rocks for fine views.

Warnings:

Take great care in and around the quarries as there are steep drops.

A short but steep descent is required to reach the Quarrymen's Hut.

Start – Lower car park (charged) at Haytor (Haytor Vale) (**765 771**). Toilets, National Park Information Centre. Refreshment van (summer).

1. Follow the grassy path directly opposite the car park entrance, heading to the right of Haytor rocks and towards the left end of rocky mounds ~0.4 miles ahead. Where the path divides a few yards from the road take the centre path of three (not left to the tor).
2. The path merges onto a stony track which reaches a gate by a large heap of rocks. Go through the gate (**7703 7745**) into **Haytor Quarry**. Follow the narrow path left with care as there is a steep drop to part of the quarry. The path leads to the picturesque pool, an ideal spot for a sheltered picnic.

Once through the gate you find yourself in a different world to the tors and moorland that epitomise Dartmoor. In what once was a hive of industrial activity, sheltered by the huge rock faces is an oasis of serenity, beauty and wildlife. Newts and dragonflies can often be spotted here and in summer water lilies add to the pool's beauty.

Haytor Quarry

Haytor Quarry was worked from the late 18th century but was busiest in the mid-19th century. Granite from here was used on a number of iconic London buildings, including the British Museum and the old London Bridge. The last stone to be extracted was used for the Devon County War Memorial, which was unveiled in 1921. Part of the quarry is now flooded and at the edge of the water is a metal winch which despite standing here for over a century still turns, albeit somewhat noisily. A large piece of timber with metal fittings on one end lying at the edge of the pool was once part of a crane used in the quarrying operations.

3. Continue through the quarry, leaving by a gate at the top end and following a grassy path NW across the moor towards Smallacombe Rocks, Greator Rocks and Hound Tor.
4. Stay on the main path as it crosses others, then take the left fork after ~300 yards, soon reaching the **Haytor Granite Tramway** at a set of points where the line divides (**7571 7773**).

The tramway was built by George Templar, owner of the Stover Estate, who had won the contract to supply granite from Haytor & Holwell quarries. It ran for 8½ miles to the Stover Canal at Ventiford, from where stone was taken by barge to the port of Teignmouth. Trains typically comprised of 12 wagons with 18 horses, who were positioned at the rear for the descent and at the front to haul them the 1,300 feet back up to the quarries.

5. Take the right fork (straight on from the path), following the Holwell branch of the tramway as it descends towards Holwell Quarries.
6. ~100 yards before the tramway bends right, to the left of the track is an abandoned unfinished or broken **apple crusher** (**7551 7773**).

Carved from granite to crush apples for cider, this is one of a number of presses on and around the moor. The presses were operated by a horse pulling a stone wheel to crush apples as it rotated around the trough, which sloped inwards allowing the juice to be collected in the centre.

7. Pass through the main part of the quarry with a massive granite rock face to the left and a rocky plateau to the right. After a

few yards of narrow path there is another, smaller promontory. Below this is the **Quarrymen's Hut** (**7507 7779**) Take care descending to it. *Located amidst the spoil the small beehive shaped hut is remarkably well preserved. Its exact purpose is unclear. The sheltered position under large granite slabs suggest it may have been a refuge for quarrymen when blasting took place but it would not have held many workers. Most sources suggest that it was an explosives store, the solid roof making it quite blast proof, but it may have been simply a tool store, or place to eat lunch out of the rain.*

Quarrymen's Hut

8. The return route follows the tramway, turning left at the set of points where you joined it.
9. An optional diversion (¾ mile) can be made to **Smallacombe Rocks** (also known as Grea Tor) from where there are magnificent views across the moor, by taking a clear path after a few yards on the left. A well-preserved Bronze Age **hut circle** can be seen just before the rocks. Return to the tramway by the same path (direction of Haytor).
10. Just before the tramway enters a cutting a shallow pool is passed on the left. ~250 yards from the pool the tramway divides again. Here a **marker stone** indicates the start of the **Templars Way** footpath which follows the 18 mile route to Teignmouth. Take the branch to your right which served Haytor Quarry.
11. Follow the track around the rocky end of the quarry, past the remains of enclosures and a single tall gatepost, until reaching the outward path close to the gate and pile of stones. Follow this downhill, soon branching left onto the grassy path back to the car park. Should you wish to visit Haytor Rocks there is a path from the quarry and another back to the car park.

WALK 12

BUCKLAND BEACON & WELSTOR COMMON : 2 MILES *

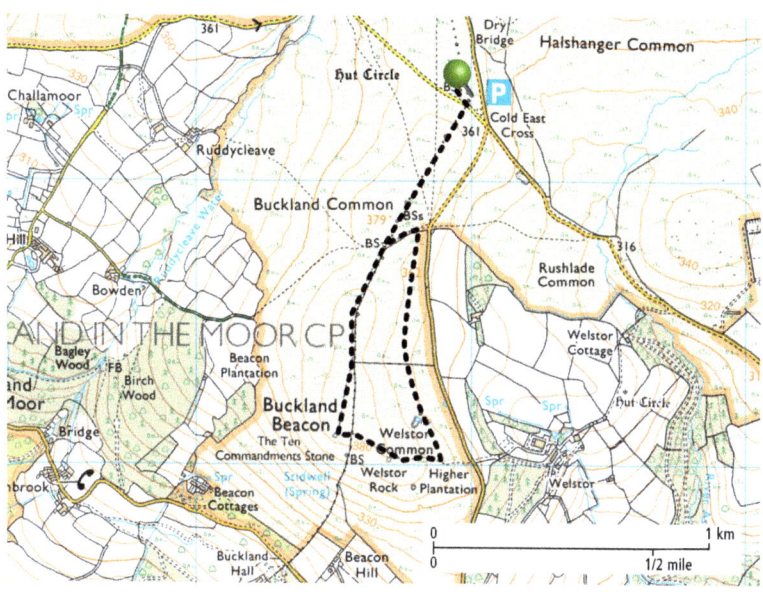

An easy walk on paths with a gentle climb to a panoramic viewpoint. The route follows a line of 19th century boundary stones and visits the Ten Commandments Stones, returning past a mysterious ruined building. This makes an ideal family walk and children in particular may enjoy discovering the stones and deciphering their inscriptions.

Start – Cold East Cross car park (**7404 7423**) on the road from Ashburton towards Widecombe & Haytor.

The route to the beacon roughly follows the ancient boundary between the parishes of Ashburton and Buckland, which is marked by a line of boundary stones. Many of the stones are carved with the initials EPB which stand for the charmingly named Edmund Pollexfen Bastard, whose family purchased the Manor of Buckland in 1614 and who erected the stones after the boundary was surveyed in 1837.

1. To reach the first **boundary stone** (*7399 7428*) follow a grassy path from the right (facing the road) (NE) side of the car park for ~50 yards. The stone, which is inscribed 'EPB 1837' on one face and 'A' (Ashburton) & 'B' (Buckland) on opposite faces, stands ~20 yards to the left of the path.
2. Return to the car park, cross the road and take a gently ascending grassy path. The next **boundary stone** (*7391 7416*) is soon reached. This has the same markings as the first.
3. Follow the right forks where the path divides after ~75 yards and after ~250 yards (not left towards a clump of trees). A third **boundary stone** (*7376 7392*) is found a little further along the path and 'A' & 'B' can also be seen on the opposite faces. 'EPB' is also inscribed but this is thought to be the only boundary stone not to be marked with the year.
4. A further **boundary stone** (*7373 7386*) with the same markings as the first two and an adjacent granite block is soon reached, as the path continues towards a drystone wall.
5. The final AB **boundary stone** (*7370 7377*) seen on the walk stands by the wall with a small unmarked stone close by. This is an older boundary stone.

Ten Commandments Stones

6. Continue to climb slowly as the path runs to the right of the wall. Just beyond a small group of trees which are on the opposite side of the wall, is a **Sheep Creep**, a window in the bottom of the wall which is small enough to allow sheep to pass but not cattle or horses.
7. The rocks of **Buckland Beacon** (*735 731*) are soon reached at the top of the hill. Here can be found the **Ten Commandments Stones.**

Buckland Beacon was one of a chain of hills on which fires were lit to warn of the approach of the Spanish Armada in 1588. It is said that the Armada was spotted from the summit. On two large granite slabs at the base of the tor are inscribed the Ten Commandments. These were commissioned in 1928 by the Lord of Buckland, William Whitely, who wished to celebrate Parliament's rejection of the proposed New Book of Common Prayer. The more than 1,500 letters were carved by Mr W.A. Clement from Exmouth, who slept in a shepherd's hut nearby and carried out the work in all weathers. Unsurprisingly he was given the nickname Moses. Over time Dartmoor's weather eroded the letters and restoration was carried out in 1995 and again in 2017. The latter work was undertaken by Iain Cotton, a lettering expert and conservator from Bath. It involved cleaning, re-carving some of the letters and painting them with a black paint designed to resist the beacon's extreme weather.

8. The rocks are easily climbed to enjoy panoramic views across the moor and South Devon. On one visit as we sat beneath the rocks enjoying our pasties a small girl climbed to the top and exclaimed '*you can see the whole world*'!

On higher flat rock a further inscription can be seen. This commemorates the Silver Jubilee of George V and reads: 'Buckland Beacon. A beacon fire one of a chain lit here by the Parishioners of Buckland-in-the-Moor in celebration of their Majesties' silver jubilee May 6th 1935. And the people shouted and said "God save the King".'

9. Return to the wall by a stile then turn right following a narrow path. After ~80 yards this reaches the '**Grey Mare Boundary Stone**' (*7355 7303*).

Older in appearance than the EPB stones, this unmarked pointed boundary stone is often referred to as the Grey Mare. However, it is likely that the Grey Mare stone stood a little further down the hill but was destroyed when the newtake wall was built in 1771 and that this is The Longstone, another boundary stone.

10. Return to the stile, cross it and walk the short distance to **Welstor Rocks** ahead.
11. Continue downhill on the path for ~220 yards then take a path on the left in the direction of Ripon Tor. This soon narrows as it passes through gorse (shorts not recommended), reaching a small **ruined building** (*7382 7318*) after ~200 yards.

To the left of the stone building is a former small quarry, marked as 'Old Sand Pit' on some maps. There are a number of theories as to the origin of the building. It has been suggested that it was an explosives store for the quarry but this seems unlikely as blasting would not have been carried out for a sand quarry. It may have been a store, or, as I have been told by someone who was brought up in Welstor, a home for the quarry horses. However it could have been built for Welstor Common Rifle Range, which was set up in 1861 for the use of Ashburton Rifle Volunteers and was in use until about 1900. It might of course been used by both the quarry and the rifle range.

12. The path continues through a gap in a wall (note the **iron gate hanger** on the post) then across the grassy area (once the rifle range), towards a wall beneath trees close to a parking area. Here, adjacent to a **stone stile**, is another **sheep creep**.
13. Cross the stile and turn left beside the wall until reaching the pair of boundary stones passed on the outward route. Take the first path on the right (your outward path) which returns to the car park. From the top of the slope Ripon Tor Rifle Range can be seen on the small hill to the right.

Sheep Creep

WALK 13

RIVER DART & VENFORD FALLS : 1½ MILES ****

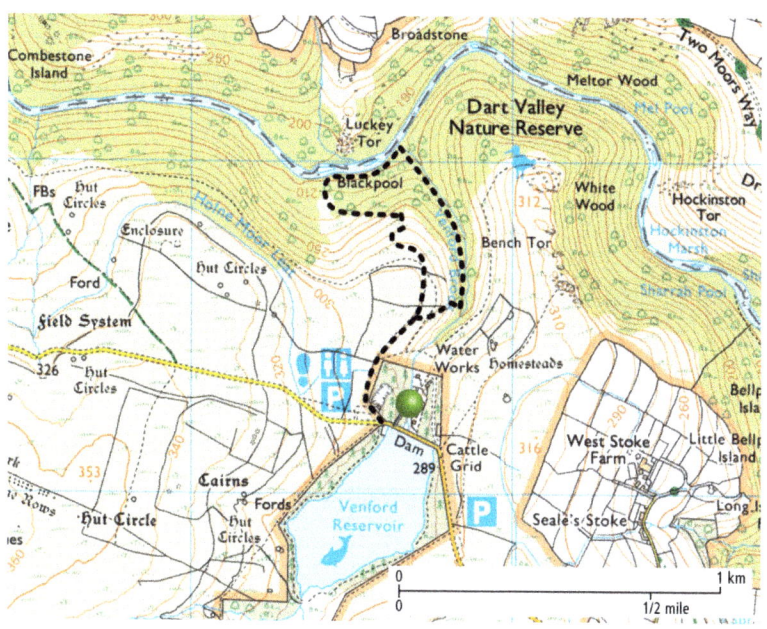

A short walk but challenging across the moor and through woods beside the spectacular River Dart and waterfalls of the Venford Brook, to one of Dartmoor's most beautiful but least known waterfalls.

Start – Venford Reservoir car park (**685 712**). Park on the Hexworthy side of the dam (far side from Holne / Ashburton). Donation box. Toilets.

Warning:

Sections of this walk are challenging, involving slippery ground, steep ascents & descents and climbing over rocks, with adjacent big drops to rivers. Appropriate footwear and great care are essential.

1. Heading away from the road follow a grassy path by a fence above trees. A **boundary stone** inscribed 'RD/H' is immediately passed.

The stone is one of 52 which mark the boundary of Venford Reservoir. They are inscribed PUDC on one side (Paignton Urban District Council) and RD/H on the other. The latter stands for 'Richard Dawson, Holne', from whom Paignton Water Works purchased 700 acres of moor, at a cost of £11 per acre. The reservoir was constructed in 1907 to supply water to Paignton and surrounding areas.

2. **Holne Moor Leat** is soon crossed on a single span **clapper bridge**. The leat takes water from the O Brook (the shortest river name in the UK and presumably the world as it obviously can't be beaten) and feeds into Venford Reservoir.
3. Where the trees end a path diverges downhill to the right, by another **boundary stone**. Don't take this but stay on the upper path which starts to bend left after ~200 yards.
4. The long bend ends after ~300 yards. From here (**6861 7169**) take a path on the right which zig zags downhill to the woods above the

Venford Falls

River Dart. On reaching the trees this bends left running just above them, before turning right again after ~250 yards and descending through a grassy area towards the river.

River Dart

5. Walk through the trees to enjoy wonderful views up and down the Dart, then turn right following a rough path above the river. Two picturesque islands are passed. Above the opposite bank is Luckey Tor. Take great care as you follow the rough path, sometimes needing to clamber over boulders, whilst enjoying wonderful views of the river below.

6. After ~300 yards the Venford Brook is reached. Follow this upstream for ~¼ mile. There are sections of path but in places you will need to climb over rocks and assess the easiest route as you walk. It may be close to the water or higher above the gorge. This is a most picturesque section of a Dartmoor stream, with successive waterfalls as the brook descends steeply to the Dart. The final waterfall reached is the unmistakable **Venford Falls** (*6885 7169*).

Concealed in the steep wooded valley, Venford Falls is one of Dartmoor's hidden gems. The brook splits into two as it cascades into a rocky pool in the dark gorge and moss-covered rocks add to the almost tropical setting. It is worth visiting both in winter when the flow is greatest and in summer when the trees are green and dappled sunlight falls onto the water. The double fall is perhaps the most beautiful of all Dartmoor's waterfalls, but although close to a road, few people visit. It is however popular with photographers and well worth taking a camera on this walk.

7. From the falls follow a narrow, steep path which ascends through the trees and meets the wider path followed outward. Turn left to return to the car park.

WALK 14

HUNTINGDON WARREN & BROAD FALLS

WALK 14A : LITTLE MAN, HUNTINGDON WARREN : 5 / 4 MILES *

WALK 14B : CONTINUES TO HUNTINGDON CHAPEL & CROSS : 6 / 5 MILES ***

WALK 14C : BROAD FALLS, HUNTINGDON CROSS, ABBOT'S WAY : 7 MILES ***

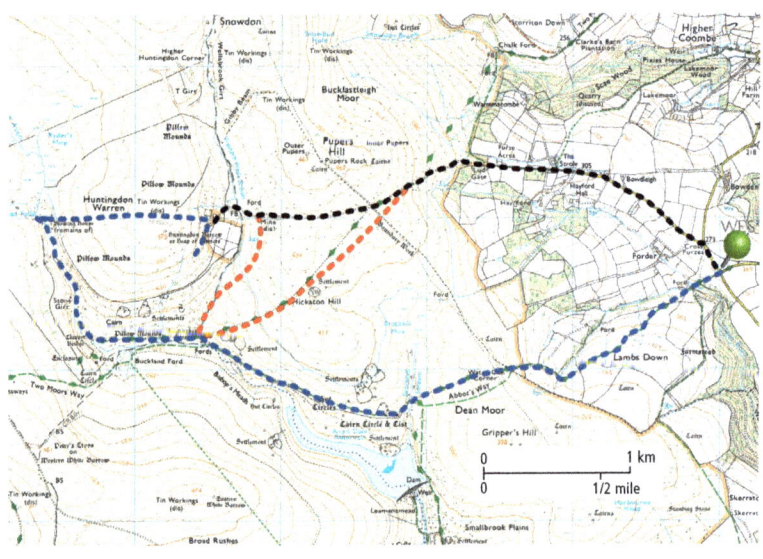

Walk 14A – An easy out and back walk along paths, although including one steady climb, exploring one of Dartmoor's historic warrens, with good views across South Devon.

Walk 14B continues along paths (some patchy) to a unique chapel, a historic cross and past Bronze Age settlements.

WALK 14

Walk 14C continues on paths (some patchy and rough) from Huntingdon Warren, passing a tiny cross commemorating an air crash, to one of the moor's hidden waterfalls, returning alongside the picturesque River Avon, then on the ancient Abbot's Way above the Avon Reservoir.

Warnings:

Take care to avoid mine shafts and pits around Huntingdon Mine.

Walk 14B - The stretch from Huntingdon Warren to the River Avon, particularly beyond the chapel, has patchy narrow paths and is often boggy (can be very boggy in winter).

Start – Parking for a few cars at 'Cross Furzes' (**7001 6663**), at the junction of the lane to Buckfast on the Wallaford Road. Follow Wallaford Road from Buckfastleigh.

Note that the exact location of Cross Furzes is ambiguous. It is known by Dartmoor walkers and in many books as where the Abbot's Way enters the moor at the junction of the lane to Buckfast on the Wallaford Road. It is however marked on OS maps and a signpost as where the lanes to Coombe & Hayford diverge ~250 yards beyond this point.

For Walks 14A & 14B, provided the ground is not too wet, it may be preferred to shorten the walk by a mile, by parking on grass to the left of the lane just beyond Bowdleigh Farm (near Hayford Hall) (**6932 6719**), ~½ mile after Cross Furzes.

WALK 14A

1. Follow the road (signed Hayford Hall, Scorriton & Combe) as it climbs gently towards the moor. After ~200 yards, at the junction marked as Cross Furzes, to the left of the lane is a **guide stone** (**6991 6670**), showing the letters 'B' (Buckfastleigh), 'A' (Ashburton) & 'T' (Tavistock). Unusually these are raised rather than incised in the stone.

2. Take the left fork (signed Hayford Hall) passing the entrance to **Hayford Hall**, after which it becomes a stony track between high banks, often festooned with wild flowers.

Old post box Hayford Hall

Hidden in trees below the moor, it has been suggested that Hayford Hall was the inspiration for Baskerville Hall in Arthur Conan-Doyle's Hound of the Baskervilles. In the summers of 1932 & 1933 the hall was rented by American heiress Peggy Guggenheim, who hosted a literary salon here. According to 'Hayford Hall: Hangovers, Erotics and Modern Aesthetics', a collection of essays about the two summers, the mostly female writers 'challenged the sexual, textual and spiritual mores of the day'. One wonders quite what went on there!

In the wall on the right of the lane is a G VI R post box. This is no longer in use but there is still a daily collection from a newer box by the gateway to the Hall, perhaps one of the most remote in Devon. The old box is sometimes decorated for Christmas with greenery and a lighted candle.

3. Pass through **Lud Gate** at the top of the track and continue straight on along the ascending path. Take the left fork where this divides after ~200 yards immediately after crossing a small leat (may be dry) & follow the track as it climbs the slope of Pupers Hill. It divides again after ~100 yards but both branches soon rejoin. The right is preferred - don't descend left towards trees.
4. ½ mile from Lud Gate, **Little Man**, a small standing stone, is passed to the left of the track (**6779 6714**).

Also known as Kit's Stone or the Lone Piper, Little Man is a guide or boundary stone, however legend gives us another story. Many years ago when merriment on the Sabbath was strictly forbidden, a group of youngsters climbed the hill dancing to a piper. Angry at such sinfulness, God sent a blinding flash and turned them all to stone. The rocks on top of Pupers Hill are the dancers and Little Man the piper. Looking back there is a superb view over South Devon.

5. Take the right fork when the track divides a few yards beyond Little Man (the left will be your return path on Walk 14B) and continue straight on after 200 yards where it crosses the **Cumston Road**, an ancient track from South Brent to Hexworthy. Continue on the track over the rise between Pupers Hill and Hickaton Hill, then ahead in the valley is **Huntingdon Warren**.

6. Follow the track down the hill passing extensive workings of **Huntingdon Mine** on the left. Towards the bottom of the valley, just to the left of the track, by a deep pit and large mound (the final mound, ~100 yards from the river) is a circular rock, flush with the ground, with a cylindrical hole cut in it. This is a **horse whim**.

Known as Avon Consols on opening in 1854, then as Devon Wheel Vor, after a period of closure it reopened as New Huntingdon Mine in 1864. Tin was mined at several levels and the engine shaft sunk to a depth of 64 metres. It closed for good in 1868 but extensive workings remain. The whim operated by a horse walking in circles to turn a shaft in the hole, which powered a pump to extract water from the engine shaft in the adjacent pit.

7. Cross a five-slab single-span clapper bridge which is adjacent to a ford. The ground around here is generally wet. Stay on the track heading diagonally left into the warren's enclosures (**665 669**). It is worth spending a while exploring the warren and contemplating life in one of Dartmoor's most remote dwellings.

The first Huntingdon Warren house was a two storey thatched building constructed in the early 19th century by Thomas Mitchelmore. Rabbits were successfully farmed, miners working on the moor providing a ready market, but the original house was largely destroyed by fire in 1890. Its replacement, constructed at a cost of £34, remained in use as a warren until after WW2, but after being abandoned was burned down by naval cadets in 1956. For much of the first part of the 20th century the warren was run by John (Jan) Waye and his wife Caroline (Carrie), who raised their family here. As the price for rabbits fell Jan supplemented their income with employment at Red Lake and Left Lake china clay works, where he looked after the horses.

The final resident of the warren, Frederick Symes, was an interesting character. He apparently used to correspond with the Abbot of Buckfast in Latin but also wrote to himself. Mr Symes, or Mooroaman as he liked to be called, would go down to Buckfastleigh Post Office, where he'd post a self-addressed letter so that the postman had to walk across the moor to deliver it next morning. It's said that after attending market and spending the day drinking Symes would often fall asleep on the way back, but his faithful horse knew the way so well that he'd bring him home safely. The remains of the cart used by Mr Symes (and maybe his predecessors at the warren) can be seen behind a gate by the site of the warren house.

8. Walk 14C diverts here. For Walks 14A & 14B return to the bridge over the Western Wella Brook (also known as the Walla Brook). For the out & back Walk 14A return along the outward route.

Walk 14B
9. For Walk 14B, 100 yards after the bridge turn right onto a narrow path to the left of a mound (by the horse whim seen earlier) and running between the remains of stone mine buildings.
10. Continue with care on the narrow indistinct paths above the mine workings looking for **Huntingdon Chapel** (**6660 6660**). This lies in a dip in a small raised area ~50 yards above the stream and ~100 yards beyond a dry leat that runs roughly in line with the most southerly wall of the warren (across the river).

A simple affair, the open air-chapel comprises stone walls, a seat at one end and an incised cross at the other. It was built early in the 20th century by a group of young clergymen who used to camp near Huntingdon Warren each summer. They named the spot Matins Corner and held services each morning. Like the warren, from where they got supplies of bread, eggs, milk plus the odd rabbit, the young men received a daily postal delivery. Each year they dammed the stream, making a pool to bathe in and to catch trout. The chapel was named after one of the clergymen, William Keble Martin, who is best known for The Concise British Flora. Cards & flowers are often left here as tributes and it is a tranquil place to say a prayer or give thanks for the beauty of the moor. A wooden plaque has been placed in the chapel fairly recently and reads:

Keble Martin open air Chapel 1903
Divine worship last held here 11th July 1982
Thou God Seest Me Gen. 16 v13

11. Continue for ~75 yards to the remains of a narrow rectangular stone building (**6658 6651**). This is the **wheel-house** of Huntingdon Mine and housed a wheel which operated the pumps to prevent the shafts from flooding.
12. Follow small paths by the stream for a further ~¼ mile (likely to be boggy) until reaching the River Avon, which on Dartmoor is also known as the Aune. A single-span **clapper bridge** crosses the Western Wella Brook just before it enters the Avon.

Dartmoor's newest clapper bridge was built over the Western Wella Brook, allowing walkers to negotiate what could be a difficult crossing. A small plaque on the bridge states that it was erected in 2018 by Dartmoor National Park Authority, funded by legacies made to Totnes Ramblers & S. Devon Ramblers.

13. Cross the clapper to visit **Huntingdon Cross** (**6646 6618**) (Walk 14C), which stands by a wall. From this point either Walk 14B or Walk 14C (from 24) can be followed back to the starting point.
14. For Walk 14B follow a path running by the River Avon, which divides ~50 yards downstream from the Wallabrook. Take the left fork which gently ascends Hickaton Hill. This is part of the **Two Moors Way** (Walk 16) but note that route is not quite the same as that shown on the OS map.
15. The path runs between Bronze Age settlements, the most complete being **Biller's Pound** immediately to the right (**667 662**).

*Inside the substantial banks of Biller's Pound are the remains of six Bronze Age dwellings, (although they are not easy to discern), with a further ten hut circles outside. Several of the best-preserved hut circles are passed either side of the track and there is another just outside the southern edge of the pound. The remains of a tinners' building is set into the wall on the SE side of the pound but is difficult to find (**6673 6613**).*

16. The path crosses Cumston Road as it descends from Hickaton Hill, then rejoins the outward Huntingdon Warren track close to Little Man. Follow this back to Lud Gate and off the moor.

Moorside Cottage, just beyond Hayford Hall, was home to Jan & Carrie Waye after they left the warren in 1939. My father once met Mrs Waye here, who told him about life at Huntingdon Warren, and later we both met her daughter Stella (then Mrs Coles) who was brought up at the warren and used to ride her pony to school in Coombe.

17. Return down the lane to your parking place.

WALK 14C

18. Follow Walk 14A to Huntingdon Warren (8). Leave the warren through the gate in the north wall by the site of the house and large sycamore tree, reaching a path after ~30 yards (or walk round the walls if the gate is locked). A number of **pillow mounds**, artificial earth mounds where the rabbits lived, can be seen above the warren.

19. Turn left on the path which soon bends right & uphill. After ~150 yards two large boulders are seen to the left of the path (SW of the warren). On the far side of the larger of these (on the rock itself) is **Huntingdon Warren Cross** (**6642 6680**), perhaps the smallest on Dartmoor.

Huntingdon Warren Cross

On October 13th 1945 an American Douglas C-47 Skytrain crashed near

WALK 14

Huntingdon Warren in thick mist. The plane had set out from Germany and had planned to land at Exeter Airport but in poor visibility the pilot was told to proceed to Westonzoyland near Bridgewater. Unfortunately he was given an incorrect bearing and the plane ploughed into the hillside near the warren house. A police search party found the wreckage the following day but sadly all seven servicemen on board had perished on the moor. In 1985, a small cross, just two inches high, was made in school by Brett Sutherland and fixed to a boulder above the warren house as a tribute to those who died in the crash.

20. Return to the warren gate then take a path heading directly up the hill (W). The path ascends to a cairn on summit known as either **Huntingdon Barrow**, or more commonly **Heap of Sinners** (*6621 6690*), from where a view opens up into the wilderness of Southern Dartmoor.

Probably of Bronze Age origin but possibly simply a pile of stones, the cairn has been much altered over the last century. Its height was reduced by 30cm between surveys in 1977 and 1995 as a result of stones being moved to build a marker cairn and two makeshift shelters. Prior to that Frederick Symes was thought to have wandered up from Huntingdon Warren and rearranged some stones from time to time, a practice started by visitors even earlier. A local newspaper report of 1946 quotes Dartmoor authority R. Hansford Worth - "It was known as, Huntingdon Barrow, alias 'The Heap of Sinners' – It certainly has been heaped by sinners, feeble-minded persons, who some years ago built it up into a grotesque cone." The derivation of the Heap of Sinners name seems unknown. Maybe more petrified Sunday dancers?

21. The path divides immediately after the cairn. Take the right fork (W) and follow this (may be boggy initially) as it descends toward **Broad Falls** (also known as Broadafalls) on the River Avon. The conical spoil heap at Red Lake is initially to the left of the path but as it bends left this forms a good marker to head towards should the path be missed and when it disappears approaching the falls.

22. A well-preserved tinners' **blowing house** is passed on the left just before reaching the falls (*6542 6692*). A small hearth chimney can be seen.

Huntingdon Clapper

Particularly impressive when the river is full, Broadafalls is a most attractive spot where the River Avon runs over granite boulders as it comes off the high moor and into the valley. It is worth walking to the top of the falls although the ground is quite rough. If the river is low it can be crossed here, maybe using one of several islands. There was once a small wooden bridge, erected by Mr Waye from Huntingdon Warren who used it to reach Redlake china clay works. By the top of the far bank are the remains of another blowing house. The moor beyond here is miry, wild and largely featureless.

23. Follow a path downstream on the left bank walking through the picturesque Avon valley. After ~¼ mile (by a lone tree) the path runs through a **vermin trap (*6551 6667*)**.

Weasels and stoats are natural enemies of rabbits and around Dartmoor's warrens were often found vermin traps that sought to catch them. The two parallel stone sides contained slots which accommodated shutters that were closed by a trip mechanism as the unfortunate creatures passed through. Once imprisoned they awaited the warrener and his terriers, with inevitable consequences.

24. Continue to **Huntingdon Clapper** (*6571 6620*), for centuries an important crossing for walkers and those working on the moors.

Huntingdon Cross

It is thought that the bridge was constructed by one of the warreners in order to give them easier access to Ivybridge and although most Dartmoor clapper bridges originate from medieval times, marks in the granite suggest that more modern cutting techniques were used here. For some years one span was missing, having been washed off by floodwaters, but this has now been replaced.

25. Staying on the left bank, the path, which may be rough and boggy in places, is followed for a further ½ mile until reaching a short stone wall close to the confluence of the Avon & Western Wella Brook. Cross a stile to discover **Huntingdon Cross** behind the wall (*6646 6618*).

The origin of the relatively small Huntingdon Cross is uncertain. It may initially have been a way marker for the Abbot's Way path but is more likely to have been placed here around 1550 as one of four boundary markers utilised by Sir William Petre to mark the extent of the Manor of Brent. This was originally part of the lands of Buckfast Abbey and came into his possession soon after the Dissolution in 1539.

26. Cross the Western Wella Brook on the **clapper bridge** (Walk 14B). Just beyond here are two **stone pillars** either side of the Avon. Short lengths of pipe protrude and I recall in the 1970s seeing the pipe in place and a grill beneath it, which was intended to prevent debris from flowing into the reservoir.

27. Continue on the path running just above the river (not the left fork after ~50 yards taken by Walk 14B). Take the left fork where

the path divides after 0.4 miles just before the top of the **Avon Reservoir**.

The river was dammed in 1957, forming a reservoir to help supply the ever increasing demands of South Devon and its holidaymakers. It is an attractive lake but a matter of opinion whether the reservoir enhances or spoils the moor. Submerged beneath the water are a number of Bronze Age hut circles, a fine blowing house and the remains of a summer retreat used by the monks from Buckfast. The central spillway on the concrete dam stands 94 feet above the river's original level and holds back up to 305 million gallons of water.

28. The path climbs gently above the reservoir then after ~½ mile descends to Brockhill Stream, which is crossed at Brockhill Ford (**6790 6579**). Continue straight on as the path ascends to the left of the summit of Gripper's Hill. There are superb views of coast and moor. You are walking on the **Abbot's Way** which is followed off the moor.

The most famous of Dartmoor's ancient tracks, the Abbot's Way linked Buckfast and Tavistock Abbeys. Also known as the Jobbers Path (jobbers were traders in wool and cloth), its origin is unclear. Whilst it is more romantic to think of monks making a path and walking across the moor to visit brethren in other abbeys, it seems more likely that jobbers formed the route with their packhorses.

29. Descend to and pass left of a small plantation, **Water Oak Corner**, then go through a gate. The path now crosses private land and signs ask walkers not to stray from it. It is part of **the Dartmoor Way**, a recently signed 108 mile circular route connecting settlements around the edge of the moor. A tiny stream is crossed in a gulley, then after a pleasant walk over Lambs Down it descends into the wooded Dean Burn valley.

30. The stream is crossed on the 18th century **Dean Burn Clapper Bridge**, a lovely spot, especially in autumn colours. One side of the bridge is inscribed '**1872**' and the other less distinctly '**1705**'. The ancient lane climbs through the trees and soon reaches your starting point on Wallaford Road where the Abbot's Way leaves the moor.

WALK 15

CORRINGDON BALL TOMB & KNATTABARROW POOL

WALK 15A : DIAMOND LANE, CORRINGDON BALL CHAMBERED TOMB & STONE ROWS : 3½ MILES **

WALK 15B : CONTINUES TO THREE BARROWS, KNATTABARROW POOL & ZEAL TRAMWAY : 7½ MILES ***

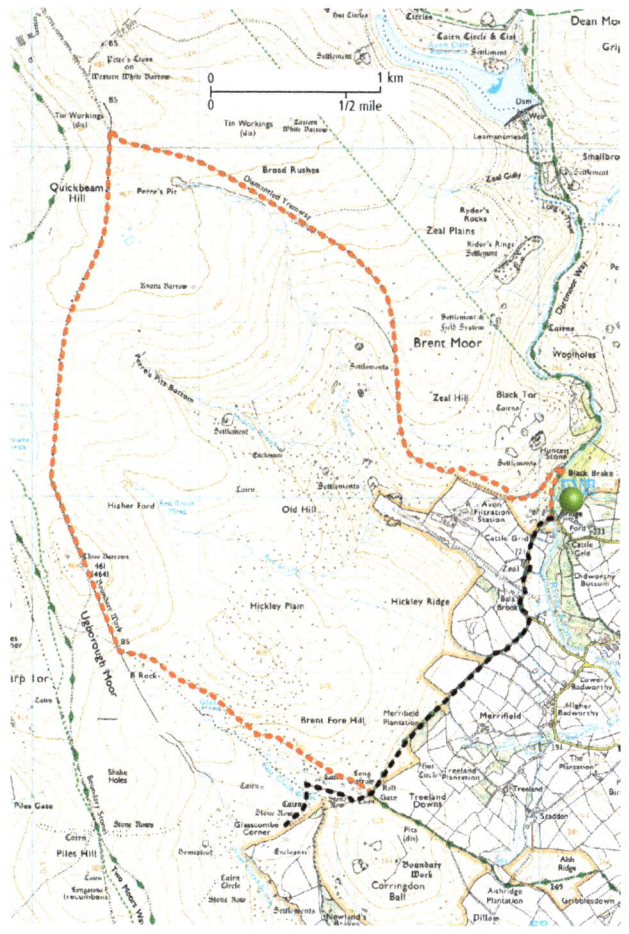

Walk 15A - A walk on paths following an ancient route to the moor, visiting Neolithic and Bronze Age remains.

Walk 15B continues on paths (some rough and maybe miry) to one of Dartmoor's best viewpoints and one of its most mysterious pools, returning along the route of a most unusual railway.

Warning:

The upper 100 yards of Diamond Lane is quite steep, rocky, rough walking and care is needed, especially when wet.

Walk 15B – Some of the paths are usually miry. The ground around Knattabarrow Pool is very rough and often wet.

Start – Shipley Bridge car park (**680 629**), near South Brent & Didworthy. Signed Avon Dam. Toilets. Charged. Refreshment van summer.

Shipley Bridge is a picturesque spot on the River Avon. The stone walls at the edge of the car park were once part of 19th century naptha works, which processed peat brought from Red Lake along the Zeal Tor Tramway. After the venture failed they were converted for drying china clay from Bala Brook Head, another enterprise that didn't last long. A leat was constructed to take water from the Bala Brook to the naptha works and later used to transport the china clay slurry to Shipley Bridge, where it was separated in pits, cut into blocks and dried.

Walk 15A

1. Turn right (W) from the entrance of the car park, following the lane downhill towards Didworthy. This crosses the picturesque Bala Brook on **Zeal Bridge** then bends left. At the end of the bend, 150 yards from the bridge, take a track on the right (**6793 6231**)(signed bridleway) which heads uphill through trees. This is **Diamond Lane**.

WALK 15

Diamond Lane

An ancient route to the moor, Diamond Lane was once part of the monastic track from Buckfast Abbey to Plympton Priory. It was used for taking ponies to and from the moor and is still designated as a bridleway, although a sign at the top sensibly advises riders to dismount. It is said that a coach and four was once driven up the lane and that the 17th & 18th century militia marched through here en route to Plymouth from Exeter, however centuries of water running off the moor eroded the track to a more challenging ascent. Remedial work has restored a good surface on the lower section but above this it is necessary to pick ones way over often slippery rocks, so great care is needed. Passing under trees and between moss-covered walls, Diamond Lane nevertheless makes a most romantic approach to the moor.

2. On the lower part of the track, just after a gate on the left, is a **stone trough** (*6791 6222*).

The origin of the abandoned moss-covered granite trough is unknown. With no water source to fill it and the River Avon not far away, it does not appear to have been placed here to water horses.

3. ~250 yards from the road pass through the gate to the moor, cross **Badworthy Leat** and continue straight on along a path beside a stone wall (passing between two walls for a short

Corringdon Ball Chambered Tomb

distance). Stay on the path when the wall twice deviates to the left, returning to the wall after ¾ mile where it meets another track at the **Ball Gate** (*6702 6129*).

Once the gate to Brent Manor Estate, Ball Gate is an imposing entrance to the moor with stone balls on the head of each post. The track through here is known as the Jobbers' Path from the men trading in wool and cloth who carried their goods over the moor.

4. Continue following the wall for a short distance to some large granite slabs, the remains of a Neolithic burial chamber, **Corringdon Ball Chambered Tomb** (*6695 6129*).

Marked on OS maps as a long barrow, this Neolithic chambered tomb is one of the largest burial monuments on the moor. Although badly damaged it is still an impressive monument, even more so when one considers it was erected here in the region of 6,000 years ago. The stone chamber, placed within the wider end of a long barrow earth mound, consists of five large slabs. Only one of these is still in the erect position and another lying on the edge of the remains of the mound may be the capstone.

5. Walk 15B departs here, whilst Walk 15A explores Bronze Age stone rows. To find the first of these continue parallel to the wall

for ~50 yards where **Corringdon Leat** is met. This comes off the East Glaze Brook near its source and supplies Corringdon farmstead.

6. Cross Corringdon Leat, then immediately follow a dry leat which runs roughly parallel. After ~100 yards this meets a **double stone row** (*668 613*). Most of the stones are small but it is usually clearly visible descending to the stream below.
7. Follow the stone row downhill to the East Glaze Brook stream. This is an attractive spot with small cascades. Cross at or by a ford and follow a track ascending the far bank, reaching another complex of **stone rows** after ~100 yards (*667 612*).

The complex of Bronze Age stone rows and cairns between the East and West Glaze Brooks is unusual in that it consists of seven parallel lines. The northernmost row is single, 157 metres in length, with stones at irregular intervals and terminates in a cairn. Two shorter triple rows run parallel, again ending at a small cairn. These may originally have been longer with stone robbed for building nearby newtake walls. Vegetation obscures some stones and careful exploration is required to get a full picture of the monument.

8. Return by the outward route, remembering to follow the straight path back to Diamond Lane and not descend where the wall deviates right.

Walk 15B

9. Follow Walk 15A to (4). Return to the Ball Gate (you may first wish to visit the stone rows described in 15A) then take the Jobbers' Path, which continues from the gate slightly left (NW) running up the East Glaze Brook valley, parallel with Corringdon Leat. The start of the path may not be clear but it is easily picked up after a short distance.
10. After ~0.4 miles the path runs in a short sunken section as it passes through a rocky area. ~200 yards beyond this is a tinners' gulley in which a lone tree stands. Don't take the narrow branch to the gulley but stay on the path 50-100 yards above it.
11. The path divides ~300 yards beyond the gulley and maps can be

Knattabarrow Pool

confusing. The Jobbers' Path runs to the right, to the ridge between Three Barrows and Wacka Tor, but neither the path nor the tor is shown on the 1:25,000 Explorer OS Map. The left fork runs above Glaze Brook Head, and crosses a reave (prehistoric field boundary) by a boundary stone to the left of the summit of Three Barrows.

12. Take the left fork, heading west towards the low point of the ridge ahead. The path passes through an area of rough grass above Glaze Brook Head and can be boggy but is reasonably distinct. If you do miss it aim for a low **boundary stone** on the reave ahead (**6550 6215**).

The stone is one of eleven marking the boundary between the parishes of Ugborough and South Brent. More are seen by the path followed beyond Three Barrows.

13. On reaching the reave by or just left of the boundary stone, turn right and follow it to the summit of **Three Barrows** (**653 626**).

The highest point in this area of Dartmoor, Three Barrows commands superb views into the moor, across Devon and to Cornwall. The tall stones at the northern end of Stalldown Stone Row (Walk 18) can be seen on the hill the other side of the River Erme. A trig point stands at the top of the hill, where as the name suggests there are three burial cairns. At 40 metres in diameter, one of these is the largest on Dartmoor. Perhaps such monuments and vantage point were reserved for only the most important Bronze Age people. In March 1944 an RAF Wellington Bomber crashed on Three Barrows, after drifting of course en-route from Dorset to Morocco. Tragically all four crew members perished.

14. Continue straight on (NNW) along a path, running just left of the centre (largest) of the 3 cairns and close to the reave. The reave ends after 0.3 miles from which point a clear path heads due north. To the left is the Redlake Tramway (Walk 16) on which a bridge can be seen at Left Lake.
15. Follow the path passing more **boundary stones**. It is a clear path but sections are usually boggy especially in wet weather.
16. After ~0.9 miles, close to a boundary stone which stands on the left of the path (**6542 6449**), are several earth mounds (one just right of the path, others ~100-200 yards to the right). Leave the path here and head right across rough ground to the mounds. **Knattabarrow Pool** is found behind the mounds (**656 645**).

Formed from china clay extraction, the dark and mysterious Knattabarrow Pool has its own legend. A peat cutter known as Peter the Peat Man, not the brightest of young men, lived in the village of Ugborough. One night he dreamt that a beautiful lady beside a pool was beckoning him, but awoke before her identity was revealed. Soon after, while walking back from peat cutting he passed Knattabarrow Pool and realised that this was the place where he had seen the girl. The next day, dressed in his Sunday best, he returned to await her but after downing a flagon of ale soon fell asleep. A group of youngsters from South Brent were also walking on the moors and one girl decided to rest at Knattabarrow Pool while the others picked whortle berries. Pete awoke from his slumber, saw the pretty young lady by the pool and realised that his dream had come true. She wasn't quite so pleased on being told that he'd been expecting her and had come claim her. Unfortunately for the Peat Man she went to find her South Brent friends and as Pete was leaning over the pool to check his reflection, two of the lads picked him up and hurled him into the dark water. The South Brent youngsters mocked Pete, saying "You're knatt a burrowing our girls" and hence the pool got its name. You may however prefer to believe that it was simply named after Knatta Barrow, a cairn on a hill SE of the pool.

17. Return to the track and continue a further ⅓ mile. Soon after it starts to ascend another path is crossed. This is the **Zeal Tor Tramway** (*6548 6508*). Turn right onto the tramway which is followed for the next two miles.

The Zeal Tor Tramway was constructed to carry peat from Red Lake Mires to the works at Shipley Bridge and opened in the late 1840s. It was a most unusual railway, with five foot gauge wooden rails spiked to granite sets. Trains were horse drawn with the horses probably hitched at the rear to slow it on the steep descent towards Shipley Bridge. The peat cutting operation failed after only a few years but the line was later used to service the china clay extraction at Bala Brook Head.

18. A number of points of interest can be seen on the gradual descent. **Petre's Pits** (*659 648*) from where china clay was extracted and taken off the moor by the tramway, is soon seen on the right. A **two mile marker stone** (*6610 6488*) stands on the left of the track ~0.4 miles after you joined it. ¼ mile beyond this is a ¾ mile marker stone (*6645 6486*). The remains of numerous **iron spikes** which secured the rails to granite sets can be seen, the best two examples (*6699 6430*) protruding several inches. Several **china clay channels** can be seen both sides of the tramway and **Bronze Age settlements** and the pretty **Bala Brook** valley are to the right.

19. Approaching Avon Filtration Station, at the corner of a field the track disappears amongst gorse. This was once part of **Zeal Tor Warren**. Continue straight on, staying 50-100 yards from the wall and reach a tarmac road after ~275 yards. Follow the road downhill (left) for ¼ mile until it reaches the Avon Dam access road. On the right of the corner is **Hunters' Stone**.

The flat-topped granite boulder known as the Hunters' Stone holds names of four Masters of the Hunt which were inscribed in the late 19th century, plus others added more latterly. It was commissioned by the owner of Brent Moor House which once stood by the river. The stone was moved to its current site in 1954 to prevent damage by construction vehicles for the Avon Dam.

20. Turn right onto the road, passing a **waterfall** and reaching Shipley Bridge after ~250 yards.

WALK 16

SPURRELL'S CROSS & CUCKOO BALL
BURIAL CHAMBER : 6½ MILES **

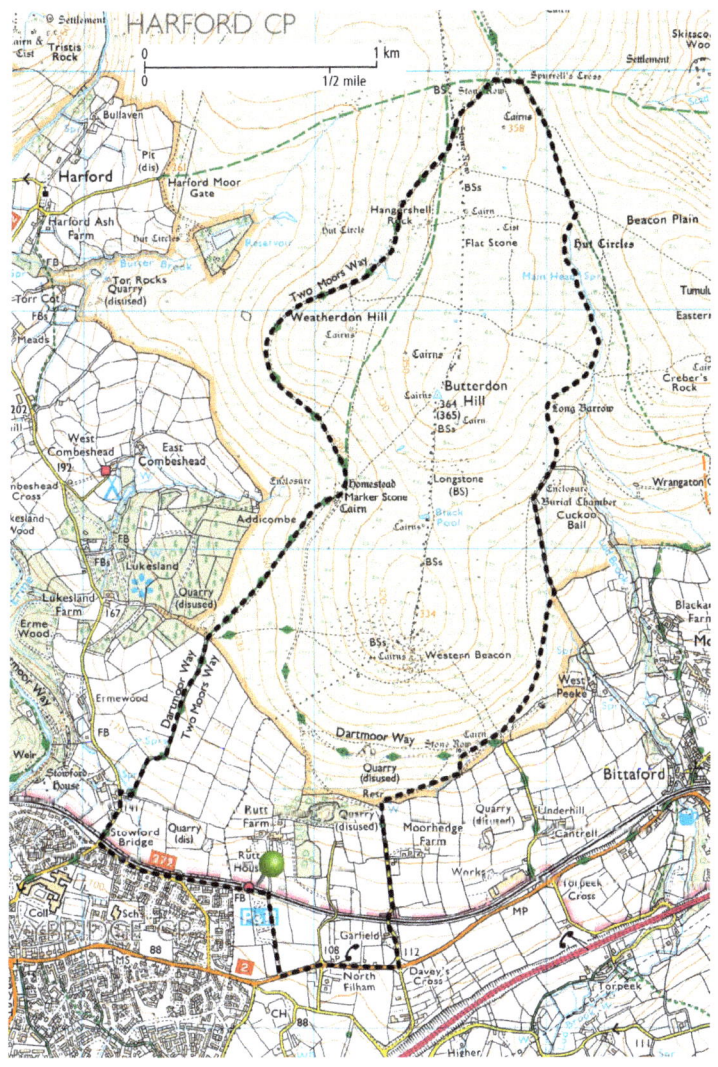

A circular walk from Ivybridge station across Harford Moor and along a disused tramway to one of Dartmoor's most distinctive crosses, returning via a prehistoric burial chamber. All on paths, although part of the return route may be patchy. Steady climb. From Spurrell's Cross there is an option to return over the hills following part of Walk 17B.

Start – Ivybridge station or station car park (charged)(**647 565**).

The first secret of this walk is that it can be accessed by train. Day trips are possible from as far away as London & the Midlands. The original Ivybridge station closed in 1965 but a new station slightly to the east opened in 1994 and is conveniently situated for the moors.

1. Turn right from the station following a tarmac path alongside the railway to Cole Lane. Turn right along the road, reaching Stowford Bridge over the railway after ¼ mile.
2. Turn right, crossing the bridge and following Harford Road for 250 yards to Stowford Farm. A standing stone can be seen in a field (private land) through the first gate on the right. This is not inscribed and probably a **scratching post** for livestock. Take the bridleway on the right just after the farm entrance, which climbs steadily, reaching a moor gate after ½ mile. This is the **Two Moors Way**.

The Two Moors Way is a varied route running across Devon's great moorlands of Dartmoor & Exmoor and the gentler countryside between them. Opened in 1976, it waymarked existing paths running for 102 miles from Ivybridge to Lynmouth, but has more recently been linked with the Erme - Plym Trail to Wembury, making a 117 mile coast to coast walk.

3. Pass through the gate (to the left is an old quarry, now grassed over) and take the middle of three wide grassy paths, heading slightly right, not the one by the wall or the one ascending Western Beacon to the right.
4. The path heads towards the **Redlake Tramway** which it meets after ~½ mile. Take the right fork where it divides shortly before the tramway, just after passing an **inspection cover** (see overleaf).

At the intersection with the tramway there is a **marker stone** (*6513 5825*) for the Two Moors Way, inscribed 'MW 2002'.

Completed in 1910 to serve the china clay extraction works at Red Lake and Left Lake, the 3 foot gauge tramway ran for 8 miles across wild Dartmoor. Steam locomotives pulled trucks and coaches, taking workers and goods to and from the works, but not china clay as that was piped as a slurry to settling tanks. After the best clay had been exhausted the China Clay Corporation was liquidated in 1933 and the tramway track lifted the following year. The line was engineered by R. Hansford Worth, an authority on Dartmoor and prolific author, who routed it away from prehistoric remains. Known locally as the Puffing Billy, it follows contours with a gradual ascent, making it an easy if not direct walk into the centre of Southern Dartmoor.

Shortly before reaching the railway you will have passed a metal inspection cover marked 'G. Waller & Son Stroud'. This was one of 80 inspection points to the china clay pipeline and more can be seen to the left of the track as you follow it into the moor.

5. Turn left to follow the tramway, passing **Hangershell Rock**, a small tor on the hillside, after 1 mile. It was once known as Hanger's Sheil, sheil meaning shelter. A stone row can be seen descending the hill ahead and crossing the tramway.
6. ~300 yards after the stone row and ½ mile from Hangershell Rock, immediately after a low cutting and at the start of a sharp left bend in the tramway take a path (*6577 5996*) to the right. **Spurrell's Cross** (*6591 5997*) is soon visible ~200 yards from the tramway. **Spurrell's Cross Stone Row** is to the right of the path ~⅓ of the way to the cross, however only a few small stones of this double stone row can be clearly seen.

Marking the junction of two tracks, Spurrell's Cross is a fine sight, although not much of the original remains. The replacement shaft was provided by the DPA in the 1930s and one half of the head is missing. Distinctive spurs above the arms give the cross its name and are unique on Dartmoor, the only other similar example being over the porch at Ermington Church.

7. Take the path heading right (SSE) from the cross, not straight on which descends the hill. Alternative return routes, which both have excellent paths, are to go back to the tramway, then return to Ivybridge on the outward route, or by turning left off the tramway by the stone row and following Walk 17B (10) over the hills.
8. The path passes a **cairn** then runs alongside a dry ditch. After ~⅓ mile the ditch ends and a path is crossed which ascends Ugborough Beacon to the left. Don't take this but continue for ~100 yards to where a gully opens up to the right of the track. This is the source of the Lud Brook.
9. Cross to the right (W) side above the top of the gully (can be boggy) and follow a path which runs along the infant Lud Brook valley (not a fork to the right which ascends the hill). After ~⅓ mile a ford in the stream is reached (**6621 5873**). A track crosses at this pleasant spot and Creber's Rocks (also known as Claret Tor) can be seen opposite on the lower slopes of Ugborough Beacon. Do not cross the ford.

Cuckoo Ball Burial Chamber

10. Take a path initially heading W from the ford. This is just to the left of a green gulley and roughly in line with the path descending from the other side of the stream. The path bends left and after ~275 yards **Butterdon Long Barrow** (*6601 5858*), a large low mound with a few stones on top, is passed on the right, although it can be difficult to spot, especially amongst bracken in summer.
11. Take the left fork where the path divides soon after the long barrow, reaching a wall after ~350 yards. Note that there are several paths on this area of hillside and it is easy to miss the long barrow but the important objective is the wall.
12. Turn right along the wall until reaching the corner where it bends sharp left. Just inside the corner of the walled enclosure is **Cuckoo Ball Burial Chamber** (*6596 5819*). Enter through a gap in the wall and the chamber is a few yards ahead through bracken. This is a lovely spot to sit and take in the view with a patchwork of fields stretching to the South Hams coastline.

Whilst most prehistoric remains on Dartmoor are Bronze Age, a few are even older, dating from the Neolithic 'New Stone Age' era that preceded it. Cuckoo Ball is one of a number of chambered burial chambers on and around Dartmoor that date from this period. Two upright stones remain but most of the cairn that once covered the tomb was probably used in the nearby newtake walls in days before preservation of such monuments was considered important. Butterdon Long Barrow is also Neolithic. It is a large oval mound but not as impressive or easy to find as Cuckoo Ball.

13. Leave the enclosure as entered and turn left following the wall for ~¼ mile until the path divides at a grassy area by a gate. Adjacent to this is a former **gatepost** with iron hanger in place.

Redlake Railway Engine Shed

14. Take the path which bends right, away from the wall. This passes a derelict red-brick building (on private land the other side of the wall)(**6599 5735**), which was the **engine shed** for the Redlake Tramway. Soon after this is the **carriage shed** which was later modified as a pig sty.
15. The tramway is soon reached. After a short distance this widens. On the right of the tramway just before an open area cut into the hillside is **Cantrell Stone Row**, which can be hard to spot if obscured by bracken in summer.
16. To the left can be seen the earth and stone works at the top of the 700 yard 1 in 5 rope hauled **incline railway** (**6563 5706**) which connected the tramway with the GWR mainline. In the indented area to the right of the tramway are the bases of buildings that held the winding gear.
17. After a further 75 yards take a path on the left which descends towards a line of trees to the right of a row of white houses. By the trees the path passes two **stone water troughs**, the second being quite unusual (**6532 5696**).

The stone trough was built in 1866 and like many Victorian constructions seems unnecessarily ornate for its purpose. It was originally fed by a small reservoir but now appears to fill with ground water. The inscription is not easy to fully decipher but reads: 'As made by Mr John Widdecombe of Torhill with the consent of Sir W.P Carew Bart (Lord of the Manor). For the use of stock depastured on the moor. May the spring never fail. October XII MDCCCLXVI'.

18. ~75 yards beyond the trough take a path left downhill that soon reaches a gate. Pass through the gate and turn left, following a stony path downhill between trees to another gate which opens onto a lane.
19. Follow the lane downhill, taking the right fork over the railway where it divides and meeting a larger road at Davey's Cross after ~0.3 miles. Turn right along the road (there is a footway on the left hand side), which prior to opening of the new A38 dual carriageway was the main road to Plymouth. After ⅓ mile turn right at a roundabout onto the access road to Ivybridge station (signed) and car park.

WALK 17

BUTTERDON STONE ROW & THE LONGSTONE

WALK 17A : SPURRELL'S CROSS, REDLAKE TRAMWAY, THE LONGSTONE, HOBAJON'S CROSS & BUTTERDON STONE ROW: 4 MILES *

WALK 17B : CONTINUES TO BLACK POOL & WESTERN BEACON: 6½ / 8 MILES *

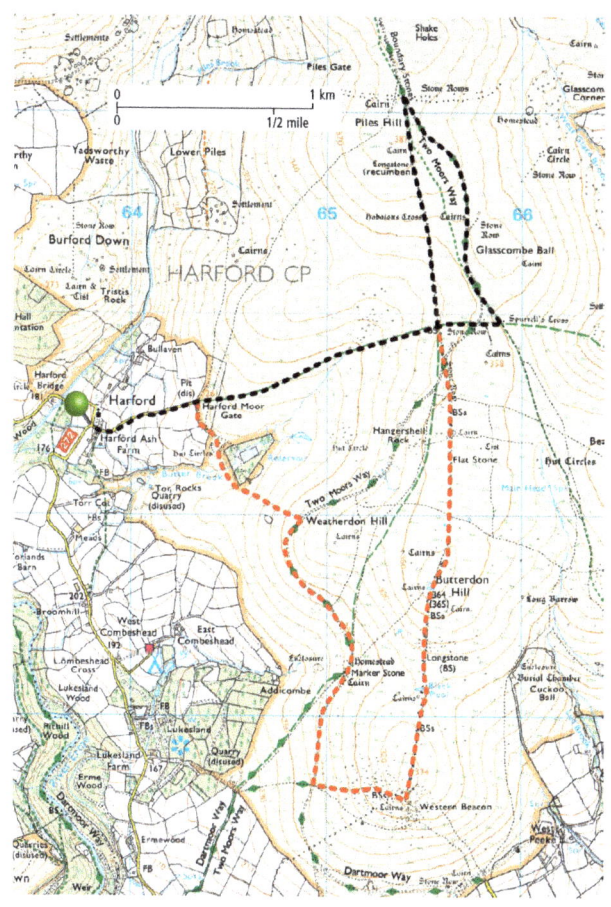

Walk 17A - A circular walk on good paths, visiting two ancient crosses, a Bronze Age menhir and one of Dartmoor's longest stone rows.

Walk 17B returns over higher ground with superb views along the Devon coast and passes two 'sacred pools'.

Warnings:

Walk 17B - The Butter Brook can be difficult to cross when water levels are very high. Diversion is suggested.

Start – These walks were intended to start from Harford Moor car park (**643 595**) but at the time of publication this was closed. There is limited parking opposite Harford church.

Alternatively Walk 17B can also be started from Ivybridge station where there is ample parking – follow start of Walk 16 to Spurrell's Cross joining Walk 17 at 3 (8 miles).

Walk 17A

1. Take the lane heading E from Harford church (right as you face the church) to the (former?) car park, an old gravel pit. Turn left from the gateway (3 posts) on the right (S) of the car park, picking up a path following the line of the lane (ENE) and running above the small plantation which surrounds the disused Butter Brook Reservoir. This is part of the **Monastic Path** which linked Buckfast Abbey with Plympton Priory.
2. Turn right after ⅔ mile at a crossroads in a rocky area, crossing **Butterdon Stone Row** with a cairn to the right and reaching the **Redlake Tramway** (Walk 16) after ⅓ mile. Cross the tramway, reaching **Spurrell's Cross** (**6591 5997**)(Walk 16) after ~200 yards.

Marking the junction of two tracks, Spurrell's Cross is a splendid sight, although not much of the original remains.

3. From Spurrell's Cross take the path running NW (looking from the cross this is the path to the right of that you came on). It

is part of the **Blackwood Path**, an ancient peat cutters' track from Wrangaton to Erme Pound. A pool, possibly a prehistoric sacred pool, is soon passed. Turn right on meeting the tramway.

4. After ~¼ mile, just before a left bend, there is a short **stone row** (**6572 6042**) ~30 yards to the right of the tramway, although with the stones lying flat this is not a particularly impressive example.

Spurrell's Cross

5. After a further ~½ mile, towards the end of a cutting, on the left of the track is a **boundary stone** (**6539 6106**). This is inscribed (although not clearly) 'U' for Ugborough Parish & 'H' for Harford Parish. Turn almost 180 degrees left (S) here onto a path that slowly diverges from the tramway.

6. After ~350 yards a menhir, the **Longstone** (**6543 6074**) is reached. *2.5 metres tall and tapering to a point, the Longstone is an impressive piece of granite which has resided on Piles Hill since Bronze Age time. The exact purpose of these prehistoric menhirs (standing stones) is not known but the Longstone may have marked the northern end of Butterdon Hill stone row that you will soon reach. It is marked on OS maps as 'recumbent' but was raised in November 2019 by Dartmoor Rangers. I'd visited on a misty day the previous month when the work was in progress and the menhir lying on the ground showing its full length. A photo in 2014 shows it standing proudly upright but by 2018 it leaned at a 45° angle. The ground is boggy and it's thought that animals pushed it over when using the stone as a scratching post. Adjacent to the menhir is a smaller boundary stone which was erected in 1803. It is of the same stone as the Longstone and may have been cut from it, meaning that menhir was once an even more impressive standing stone.*

7. The path slowly descends the slopes of Piles Hill, passing another small **boundary stone** after ~150 yards and reaching **Hobajon's Cross** (**6551 6047**) after a further ~200 yards.

Hut Circle near Butter Brook

Hobajon's Cross is unusual in that rather than the traditional construction it is simply an upright stone with a cross incised on one face. It might have once been the end stone of Butterdon Stone Row, although of course the cross would have been cut much later. This and Spurrell's Cross may have marked the route of a track from Buckfast Abbey to Plympton Priory and it may also have acted as a boundary stone.

8. At the bottom of the hill **Butterdon Stone Row** can be seen running along the path. Another **boundary stone** is passed just before the row.

Butterdon Stone Row, the second longest on Dartmoor, extends for over a mile from a cairn on Butterdon Hill to Hobajon's Cross. It comprises mostly low stones and has stretched out across the moor for more than 3,000 years. It's probably the earliest of Dartmoor's stone rows to have been documented, thanks to a map drawn in the 1400s when the Abbots of Buckfast disputed lands with 'Men of Devon'.

9. Stay on the path by the stone row for ⅓ mile from Hobajon's Cross, until it crosses your outward path (~100 yards before a large cairn & ~200 yards before meeting the tramway). For Walk 17A turn right and follow the outward path back to Harford, or for Ivybridge continue to the Redlake Tramway and take the Two Moors Way off the moor (reverse of Walk 16 outward).

Walk 17B

10. Follow Walk 17A to (9) but stay by the stone row as it crosses the tramway and continue uphill to a grass-covered **cairn** (**6565 6940**), with a hollow, a good spot to sit and look back into the moor.
11. The path continues to the summit of **Butterdon Hill** where there are two large **cairns**, a **trig point** and an amazing view to a long stretch of the South West coast.
12. Continue straight on, descending Butterdon Hill (the final part of the descent is quite steep), passing four more **boundary stones** and **Black Pool** (**6548 5813**), then ascending **Western Beacon**. More **boundary stones** are passed on the ascent. (The walk can be shortened by taking a path right to the tramway from Black Pool.)
13. There are several **cairns** on the summit, the remains of a small **quarry** and a **boundary stone** marked with an 'H' on one side and a less distinct 'U' on the other, denoting the division between Harford and Ugborough.
14. The quarry is beyond the cairns just below the far (S) end of the beacon's summit. It provides a sheltered place to stop for a while on a windy day and there is a path down on the left if you wish to explore it.
15. From the top of the quarry take a grassy path descending to the right (NW) which meets the Redlake Tramway after ~0.3 miles.
16. For Ivybridge continue straight on down the hill to the gate where you entered the moor.
17. For Harford turn right following the tramway for ~1 mile until a path on the left (**6486 5897**) above the trees surrounding Butter Brook Reservoir. The Butter Brook can be difficult to cross in winter or after periods of rain, so if in doubt remain on the tramway to the point it was reached on the outward route.
18. The path crosses the Butter Brook on stepping stones at a ford (**6447 5920**) but these are often covered, after which a fine collection of Bronze Age **hut circles** can be seen. Follow the track uphill (NW) from the reservoir back to the lane.

WALK 18

STALLDOWN STONE ROW

WALK 18A : STALLDOWN STONE ROW & HILLSON'S HOUSE : 5½ / 11 MILES **

WALK 18B : CONTINUES TO DOWNING'S HOUSE & RIVER ERME : 6½ / 12 MILES ***

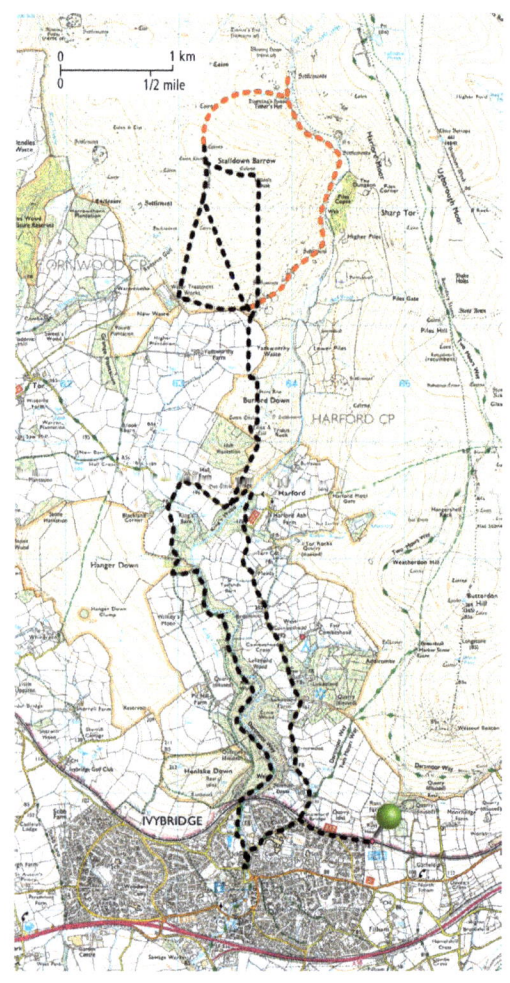

WALK 18

Walk 18A - A walk to Dartmoor's tallest stone row, perhaps the most impressive of all its prehistoric remains and to the relics of one of its legendary dwellings. Two climbs and some stretches without paths.

Walk 18B returns along the picturesque River Erme, passing the moor's best-preserved tinners' hut and the ancient Piles Copse. This route includes some rough ground without paths.

Warning:

Parts of the upper section of the path from Ivybridge to Hall Farm are quite rough, often muddy in winter and a ford near King's Barn may be impassable when water levels are very high.

Walk 18B - The ground from Stalldown Stone Row to Downing's House is rough walking.

Start – Harford (**638 694**) or Ivybridge. At the time of publication Harford Moor car park was closed. There is limited parking in the village and by Harford Bridge. Taxis can be taken from Ivybridge station to Harford.

An attractive extension to the walk following the River Erme from Ivybridge is included as an alternative. This can be shortened from the distances shown above by using lanes, particularly if starting from the station.

Walk 18A

1. **From Ivybridge** town centre follow Erme Road then Station Road, on the W bank of the Erme. Note that this refers to the old station. It is 1 mile from the new station, turning left opposite Stowford Bridge.
2. Pass Stowford Mill and pick up a path into the woods beside the river (part of The Dartmoor Way) soon passing under the railway viaduct.

The impressive 8 span Ivybridge Viaduct was built in 1893 to the design of Sir James Inglis. It replaced Brunel's original 1848 viaduct when the line was converted from broad gauge. Six piers from Brunel's bridge remain but the timber decking is long gone.

3. A most attractive series of pools, waterfalls and cascades is passed as the path heads up the river. Left of the path, 0.3 miles beyond the viaduct, is an old swimming pool.

Constructed in 1873-4 as a reservoir to supply clean water to Ivybridge, it was no longer required when Butter Brook Reservoir was established in 1914 and became a swimming pool. Changing facilities and a diving board were constructed and many children were taught to swim here. It was used by the people of Ivybridge until the 1960s and has now been partly filled in, however the old plug mechanism can still be seen.

4. Stay on the path that runs mainly close to the river for a further 1¼ miles. Go straight on at several stiles (not left up steps by the first stile). The path narrows and becomes rougher, then branches sharp left (signed Dartmoor Way), climbing away from the river.

5. A stream is immediately crossed, then a double stile into a field. Leave the field after a few yards through a gate on the right.

6. After crossing two small streams and passing through a gate the path divides with no signs. Take the left fork gently rising through the wood and soon entering a field. Follow the path right to a gap in the corner of the field, then go diagonally across the next field (not right to King's Barn).

7. From the N corner of the field a track leads to the lane at Hall Farm. This is reached by negotiating a ford prior to a gate. A very wobbly bridge (at time of writing) crosses the ford but this can flood and be impassable.

8. On reaching the lane turn right, following it for ~⅓ mile, until a gate on the left soon after a sharp left bend (~150 yards before a house which can be seen ahead). Go through the gate following instructions from 11.

9. **From Harford** take the lane heading N running beside the churchyard and soon turning sharp left as it descends to **Harford Bridge** from where there is a pretty view up the River Erme.

Harford's attractive little church in a picturesque setting is well worth looking inside. Dedicated to the Celtic St Petrock, the church dates from the late 15th or early 16th century. An ancient cross stands at the front of the churchyard, although this is not its original site. The roughly cut granite cross was moved here from Harford Moor Lane, where it was acting as a gatepost. It is assumed to have been one of the crosses marking the route from Buckfast Abbey to Plympton Priory, which enters the moor along Diamond Lane (Walk 15) and passes Spurrell's Cross.

10. Continue for a further ~275 yards until a gate on the right (*6345 5944*)(not the gate immediately after the bridge).
11. Go through the gate and follow a path which runs to the right of Hall Plantation and leads to Burford Down. Pass through a gate at the top of the plantation and turn left onto a path by the wall (not straight on to Tristis Rock, a small tor on the hillside). Note that the paths on Burford Down are not marked on the OS map.
12. The path soon bends right and after ~150 yards reaches the ⅓ mile long **Burford Down Stone Row** which starts at a **cairn circle** (*6369 6017*) in which a lone tree stands (~150 yards W of Tristis Rock). Follow the stone row, which becomes less distinct as many stones are hidden by gorse, aiming for Stalldown ahead, with circular Bronze Age settlements clearly visible on its lower slopes. The ground on the lower part of the stone row may be wet in winter.
13. On reaching a wall turn left to find an open gateway to enter the next enclosure (part of Yardsworthy Waste) then follow a grassy path parallel to the left wall for 0.3 miles.
14. Aim for the far right (NE) corner of the enclosure where a gate (*6361 6106*) leads onto the lower slopes of Stalldown.
15. From the gate cross a dry leat soon reaching a track which leads to a water intake on the River Erme and which you will join later if following walk 18B. For the next section there are two options.
16. The most direct (½ mile shorter) but steepest is to ascend Stalldown aiming slightly left of the summit (NNE). There is no path but the going is reasonable. Once the steepest section is completed **Stalldown Stone Row** (*6321 6207*) can be seen ahead. Aim for this.

Stalldown Stone Row

17. Alternatively, turn left on the track, gently climbing towards a water works building (~0.4 miles). Shortly before this the dry leat crosses the track and a partly submerged metal pipe can be seen. Just before the building is a **marker stone** with pyramidal head that is assumed to relate to the water works.
18. Turn right heading N from the track. There is no path but the leat crossing is a good starting point. Keep right of water works and left of an area of clitter. The stone row is reached after ~½ mile of mostly steady climbing but is visible well before this.

Also known as Staldon Stone Row or the Cornwood Maidens, Dartmoor's finest stone row runs for almost ⅓ of a mile, north – south across the crown of Stalldown. The most impressive stones, some up to 8 feet high, are at the northern end. Much of the row was restored in 1897 by the Dartmoor Exploration Committee, who raised most of the fallen stones but may have slightly altered their alignment as the row is no longer straight. Although not far from the edge of the moor, the controversial closure of the parking areas means that it is not so easily accessed, but perhaps this adds to the monument's remoteness. Its mystique and majesty are best experienced from the northern end, from where there is a fine view up the Erme Valley into the centre of

Hillson's House

Southern Dartmoor, with the tip of Red Lake spoil heap peeping over the hills.

19. Two thirds of the way along the stone row stands a **cairn circle** adjacent (right) to the row. Continue to the far end of the stone row, where the stones are tallest. Hillson's House can be seen on the summit of Stalldown. Walk 18B departs here.

20. For Walk 18A return to the cairn circle then head E to **Hillson's House** (**6367 6229**). This may have dropped out of view but is soon seen on the summit of the hill. A **ring cairn** or **enclosed cemetery** is passed just before reaching Hillson's House. The earth-covered stone walls form an almost perfect circle of ~25 metres diameter and are one of the many Bronze Age remains in this area.

Formed of stones from the Bronze Age cairn on the summit of Stalldown, Hillson's House is the subject of one of Dartmoor's intriguing legends. A small baby was once found on the hill and taken off the moor to safety. Efforts to locate his parents failed and he was eventually brought up by an elderly childless couple who named him Hillson, presumably son of the hill. When he grew up Hillson returned to Stalldown and built himself a small house with stones from the cairn. Here he lived for many years, earning a living from making eight-day clocks. It is of course debatable as to how much, if any, of the story is true. One could imagine the stones forming a shelter but it seems hard to believe that someone could have lived on top of the hill and carried out the intricate craft of clock making, however the respected Dartmoor writers William Crossing and Eric Hemery both suggest that there is evidence that the house did belong to a man called Hillson who made watches or clocks.

21. Turn right (S) from Hillson's House, descending Stalldown on what is initially a good path but gradually narrows, until meeting the waterworks track crossed on the ascent. You may wish to explore the pounds & hut circles close to the track (See Walk 18B, 26).
22. Return to the start by your outward route. If returning to Ivybridge you may prefer to turn left and walk down the lane to Stowford Bridge (~⅔ mile shorter than outward route). A corner is cut off by taking a path right immediately after Harford Bridge.

Walk 18B

23. Follow Walk 18A to 19 then head NE towards settlements on the opposite side of the Erme, just to the right of two gulleys (Dry Lake & Left Lake). This is hard walking with tussocky grass. The objective is **Downing's House** (*6395 6293*) close to the River Erme. It is

River Erme Weir

easiest to walk in an arc so that you avoid the steepest descent and come out at the small stream, Downing's House Brook.

This small man-made cave known as Downing's House was used by tinners to store tools. There are suggestions that an illicit still was kept here for distilling alcohol. It is also known as Smuggler's Hole, with stories that it was used to store contraband brought ashore on the South Devon coast. The granite cave has a thick covering of turf and heather, so can be missed if walking up the gulley but is easily spotted when descending.

24. Now in the beautiful Erme Valley, turn left along a track to a water intake and weir ~250 yards upstream (**6402 6315**).

This is a beautiful spot and shows that mankind's interference does not always damage the moor's aesthetics. It is one of only two places on Dartmoor where water is abstracted directly from rivers for the public water supply. The other is on the Bala Brook. Behind the weir is a clear, deep pool which invites swimming on a hot day, although great care would be needed owing to the weir and adjacent fish pass that allow salmon and trout to travel upstream to spawn. The weir was rebuilt in 1995 when the denil fish pass was added, but found to be too low to maintain a sufficient head of water to supply the intake, so was modified a year later.

25. To return, the track which serves the water intake is followed downstream, passing through a steep sided valley with **Piles Copse** on the opposite bank.

The only one of Dartmoor's three high-altitude woods situated on the southern part of the moor, Piles Copse is formed of ancient oak trees stunted and wind-twisted by the harsh weather. Beneath the trees is a carpet of moss and lichens, covering granite boulders and lower branches and forming an enchanting woodland.

26. After ~1½ miles, shortly before the track meets the point where it was crossed on the outward route, either side of it can be seen some excellent example of **Bronze Age pounds & hut circles**. The best of the pounds is to the left of the track (**638 612**) and the best hut circles to the right after a further ~100 yards.

27. Leave the track and follow the outward route through the gate and back to the lane, then to Harford or your preferred route to Ivybridge (see 22).

WALK 19

THE BANDSTAND & SHAVERCOMBE WATERFALL : 5½ MILES ***

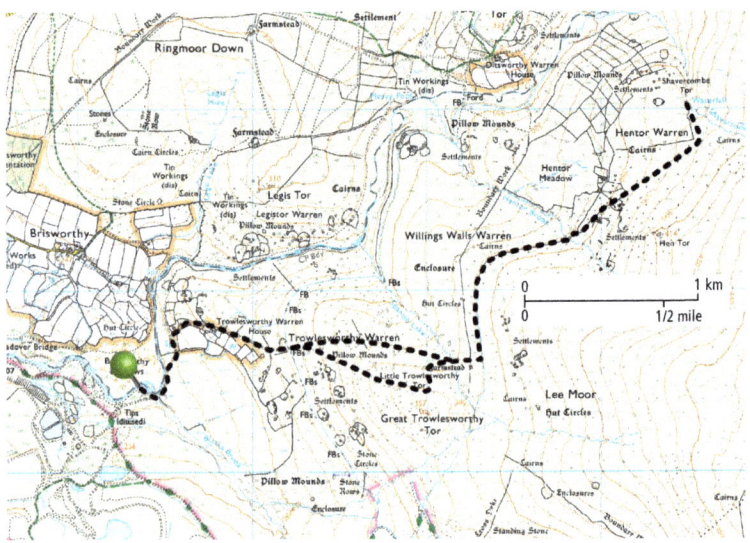

A walk across open moor to the hidden Shavercombe Waterfall, one of Dartmoor's gems, passing one of its more unusual stone relics and following a Bronze Age field boundary. Some sections without clear paths.

Start – Blacka Brook Bridge car park by confluence of Blacka Brook and River Plym (**564 644**). This is a pretty spot and quieter than nearby Cadover Bridge.

Coming from the Plympton / Shaugh Prior direction, pass the main Cadover Bridge car park on your left and take the road right, on the bend, immediately before Cadover Bridge itself. From Yelverton direction the turning is immediately left after Cadover Bridge.

Follow this road for ½ mile until it bends right and uphill. Just before the bend take the rough track left towards Trowlesworthy Warren.

1. Follow the stony track over the Blacka Brook bridge, climbing from the Plym valley towards **Trowlesworthy Warren** house and passing some hut circles & tin workings.

Trowlesworthy was probably the first of the many warrens on Dartmoor, the earliest reference to rabbits being farmed here being in a lease dated 1651 to John Hamblin, a skinner from Plymouth. It continued to operate as a warren until 1956 when Devon was declared a rabbit clearance area. The last warrener, Robert Giles, died in 1969. Trowlesworthy was owned by the Woolcombe family from 1560 until 1969, when it was left to the National Trust. The present house probably dates from the early 19th century and contains stone from the former warren house. It now operates as Trowlesworthy Warren Farm.

2. Take a vague path on the left just before the farm entrance, which soon joins a track running above the farm and its enclosures (this is often muddy), then gently climbs towards Little Trowlesworthy Tor, until meeting the **Lee Moor Leat**.

The 3 mile long Lee Moor Leat takes water from the River Plym close to Ditsworthy Warren where there is a weir and sluice. It was originally constructed to provide power for Bottle Hill Tin Mine at Plympton but later adapted to serve the extensive china clay works, where it feeds into a lake known as Big Pond.

The Bandstand & Lower Trowlesworthy Tor

3. Cross the leat on the bridge (**5720 6468**) and take a path heading diagonally right, climbing directly towards Little Trowlesworthy Tor. There are several patchy paths to the tor and some pass Bronze Age hut circles, of which there are a number on the slopes, some inside enclosures.
4. Head right of the tor to avoid the main clitter. Note a number of cut rocks on the ridge between the tors, the largest of which is known as **The Bandstand** (**5780 6448**).

The huge cylinder of granite known colloquially as The bandstand, was cut in the 19th century from a particularly fine grade of pink granite and intended for use as the base of a flagpole in Devonport Dockyard to celebrate its independence from Plymouth in 1825. The reason why it has stood between the Trowlesworthy Tors for almost two centuries varies according to sources. Some say that the plan was over ambitious as it was considered too difficult to transport the rock from the moor to the coast, others that funding did not materialise.

5. From here there are good views ahead but looking back the view is marred by Lee Moor china clay workings. The river in the valley ahead is the Spanish Lake and beyond that two **reaves** (earth & stone boundary walls) can be seen running further into the moor. These are the next objective.
6. Descend towards a sandy area on the Spanish Lake stream ¼ mile NE of The Bandstand rock (just left of a line to Hen Tor). There is generally a clear route running through a gap in the bracken towards the ford from the tor or Bandstand but the route may vary from year to year.
7. Cross the Spanish Lake at this sandy ford (**5805 6473**) and take the right fork of two tracks (which soon disappear) heading due east and uphill, reaching the first reave after 200 yards. Cross this reave and meet another slightly less distinct reave after 75 yards. These Bronze Age boundaries have been here for around 3,500 years and form useful guides for walkers.
8. Turn left, following the path on the near side of the reave. Ditsworthy Warren, another of Dartmoor's warrens, soon comes

Shavercombe Waterfall

into view on the opposite side of the Plym valley. The house still stands and was used as a location for the film War Horse.

9. The reave bends sharp right and reaches the Hen Tor Brook after ~0.6 miles. From here it is ~¾ mile to Shavercombe Waterfall in the next valley ahead but there is no clear path.

10. Cross the Hen Tor Brook and another gulley ~70 yards ahead, then continue to the left of the stone wall starting on your right below a large area of clitter. Hen Tor is above this. Many of the enclosures here belonged to **Hen Tor Warren**.

The warren originates from the late 18th or early 19th century and occupied the area of the former Hen Tor Farm. It was operated as part of Ditsworthy Warren until the 1930s. Nothing remains of the house but 58 pillow mounds (artificial earth mounds in which the rabbits made their burrows) and 4 vermin traps have been recorded. The land here is hardly conducive to cultivation and it is said that 13 oxen were needed to haul a plough.

11. When the wall (enclosure) ends continue straight on (NE). After an initial boggy area there is a semblance of path here through bracken and clumpy grass, until reaching the corner of another

Hen Tor

earth boundary after ~0.3 miles. (If the path takes you to the earthwork walk along it uphill to the corner.)

12. Turn left (N) along the boundary towards tops of trees just visible ~125 yards ahead in the valley. **Shavercombe Waterfall** (***5948 6605***) lies under the trees. Go past any steep paths that descend to the trees and continue on an easier path that doubles back to the waterfall ~100 yards beyond them.

Like most falls on Dartmoor Shavercombe Waterfall is notable neither for its drop nor volume, but it is simply a very pretty spot in a remote location. The Shavercombe Brook falling into a pool amongst trees in a steep sided gorge is one of the most delightful places on the moor.

13. Return by the outward route to the sandy ford on the Spanish Lake. (You may wish to divert to explore the remains of Hen Tor Warren.) Rather than climbing over Little Trowlesworthy Tor, take a track running to the right of the tor (and outcrop), passing through a gap in a low wall and descending to the bridge over the leat.

WALK 20

DEVONPORT LEAT, CRAZYWELL POOL & NUN'S CROSS

WALK 20A : DEVONPORT LEAT & BLACK TOR FALLS : 3½ MILES *

WALK 20B : CONTINUES TO CRAZYWELL POOL, CROSS & FARM : 4½ MILES **

WALK 20C : CONTINUES TO NUN'S CROSS & FARM, MONKS' PATH & CROSSES : 8½ MILES **

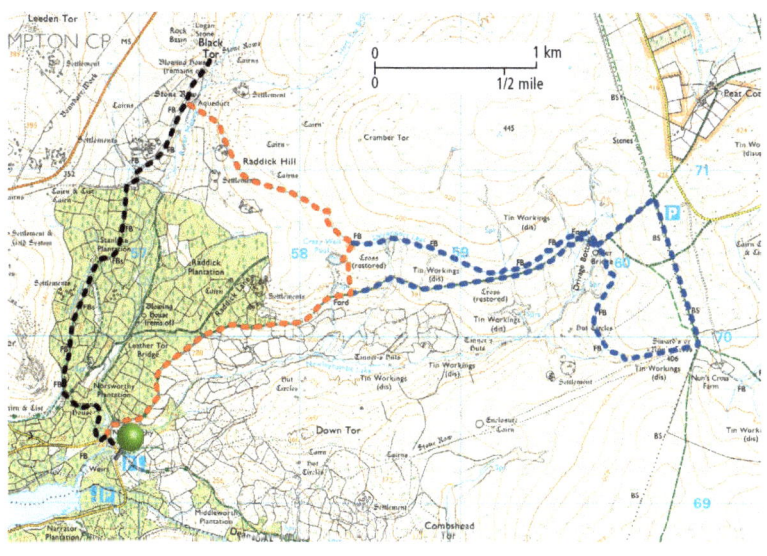

Walk 20A - A walk through woods, then on open moor along the historic Devonport Leat, passing two very different waterfalls. The entire walk is on good paths. Short climb at start.

Walk 20B continues to one of Dartmoor's most mysterious pools, a nearby cross and a long abandoned farmstead. Other than a moderately rough climb beside Raddick Falls, the walk is on good paths.

Walk 20C continues along the leat to one of the moor's most isolated dwellings and returns past several crosses on the Monks' Path. Also mainly on good paths.

Start – Norsworthy Bridge car park (**569 693**)
at the head of Burrator Lake.

WALK 20A

1. Head right (NW) out of the car park, crossing both road bridges. Take a footpath on your right, just after the second bridge (River Meavy). Go through the gate signed 'Footpath' and head upriver.
2. The path twists and turns as it moves away from the River Meavy and climbs into the woods, meeting another track after 0.3 miles. Cross this and continue ahead on the signed footpath a few yards to the left for ~30 yards until another track is met.
3. Turn right onto this track which soon meets the **Devonport Leat** as it flows under a small clapper bridge.

Constructed in 1790, the Devonport Leat is a master of engineering. It meanders across Dartmoor, descending slowly as it curves around hillsides and still serves an operational purpose. The leat originally ran for 27 miles from an intake off the West Dart near Wistman's Wood, picking up water from the Cowsic and Blackabrook streams, to what was then Plymouth Docks and became Devonport Dockyard in 1824. The operational part of the leat now feeds into Burrator Reservoir. It once fed a hydroelectric turbine at Yelverton Reservoir. Flat stones jutting out at intervals from the granite sides are 'sheep leaps'. These are for sheep to cross, or to allow a way out for any who fall in. Small trout can often be seen darting about in the clear water and with paths alongside for most of its length, following the leat makes for easy walking.

4. Turn right following a path beside the leat for 0.8 miles, a very pleasant walk through the trees, until it passes through a gate onto the open moor. The path continues beyond the gate and the ruined buildings to the right are the remains of **Stanlake Farm**.

Stanlake was one of several farms abandoned in the 1920s at the insistence of the water authorities who feared their effluent may run off into the reservoir. The remains of walled enclosures can be seen either side of the leat but the farmhouse no longer stands.

5. Continue alongside the leat for another 0.4 miles, crossing to the left bank on a small bridge after ~150 yards to avoid farm enclosures, then back to the right after a further ~250 yards. Soon in view are the **Leat Falls** and **Aqueduct** but before visiting these it's worth making a short detour to **Black Tor Falls** (*5748 7165*).

6. To do this cross back to the left side of the leat just before it bends right to the aqueduct and take a path that diverges left up the valley staying to the right of a wall (not the path further left climbing the hill). After ~275 yards, just after passing between two large rocks in a broken down wall, a narrow path descends to the falls.

7. A simple metal bridge (may not be permanent) enables walkers to cross (with care – it's wobbly) and investigate a well-preserved **blowing house** on the far bank.

The attractive Black Tor Falls, one of the most picturesque spots on Dartmoor, are well hidden in the Meuvy Valley. The blowing house door lintel is still in place and bears the (barely legible) inscription XIII, probably relating to its registration. A mortar stone (stone with depression in

Black Tor Falls

which tin ore was crushed) can be seen inside and many other tinning remains are found in the area. Another mortar stone can be seen close to the falls on the opposite bank.

8. Return to the leat. Walk 20A returns to the start by the outward route.

Walk 20B

9. Follow Walk 20A to (8) then cross the aqueduct with care. Cross the leat at the end of the aqueduct with great care and ascend the rough path on the right side of the falls. Alternatively, to avoid what can be a slippery crossing, climb up the left side of the falls were the path is rougher and cross at the first stone bridge. Look back at the leat opposite and it appears to be flowing uphill, an illusion that can be seen on a number of Dartmoor's leats.

The leat makes a spectacular sight as it descends from Raddick Hill then crosses the metal aqueduct known as Iron Bridge, which is still supported by the granite piers of the original wooden aqueduct that was built in 1792. Also known as Raddick Falls, the water drops 130 feet as it tumbles towards the River Meavy.

10. Continue walking by the leat, which bends around the head of a tinning gulley and passes through a sluice ¾ mile from the aqueduct. To the right of the leat there is a collection of cut **granite blocks**.

Grooves in the stone show that the blocks were cut by the feather and tare method, where a line of metal wedges with tapered shims (feathers) either side are hammered into holes drilled in the granite. Eventually a crack line appears and the stone splits. As this method wasn't used on Dartmoor until 1800 and the leat was built in 1790, it can be assumed that the stones were not surplus from construction and may date from renovations in the late 1800s.

11. After a further ~200 yards a **clapper bridge** is reached (*5836 7058*) which is wider than the single slabs that form most of the leat crossings. An ancient cart track once crossed here. Two more collections of cut blocks can be seen close by. From the bridge follow a path at right angles to the leat which reaches the well-hidden **Crazywell Pool** (*582 704*) after ~100 yards.

There are many legends associated with the steep-sided, mysterious body of water that is commonly known as Crazywell Pool (Crazy Well on OS maps) but also as Clazywell or Classiwell, the best known being that it is bottomless. When villagers from Walkhampton decided to check this and tied all the church bell ropes together then fed them weighted into the pool, it was estimated that their full extent of 540 feet had failed to reach the bottom. However, in the dry summer of 1844 the pool was almost emptied to supplement the Devonport Leat and the bottom found. Its depth was estimated at a mere 15 feet.

Crazywell's origin dates back to tin mining times and it is probably a flooded mine excavation. It may have a bottom but is another legend true – that the level rises and falls with the tides in Plymouth Sound? Sadly, but not surprisingly, it's not. The level is fairly constant, the pool being fed by an underground spring. Perhaps it is true that sometimes at night an articulate voice is heard calling out the name of the next person in the village to die. Or that anybody who looks into the water on midsummer's eve will see an image of the next parishioner to die. Maybe it is haunted by a witch who does nothing more sinister than offer bad advice. What is of no doubt is that the pool is popular with wild swimmers and on my first visit to plan this walk I arrived just as a naked man emerged from the water!

12. Turn left (SE) to **Crazywell Cross** (*5838 7040*), which lies ~150 yards SE of the eastern edge of the pool. Walk 20C diverges here.

For many years the cross was unnamed but more recently it has become known as Crazywell Cross due to its proximity to the pool. The head and arms are original but the fairly short shaft is a replacement, as is probably the socket stone in which it stands. It is one of a long line of crosses marking the Monks' Path, a route across the moor. There is a good view to Burrator Lake.

13. For Walk 20B turn right (SW) at the cross, heading downhill and soon reaching a stony track. This is the **Monks' Path**.
14. Turn right along the path which is followed for 1¼ miles back to Norsworthy Bridge. After ~200 yards the ruins of **Crazy Well**

Farm (*5809 7005*) can be seen just below the path. These are worth exploring.

Crazy Well Farm was first documented in 1585 but probably existed some time before this. The farmstead is thought to have been abandoned in the latter part of the 19th century when it was incorporated into the neighbouring Kingsett Farm. The door lintel of the tiny house is still in place and a dog shelter can be seen in the enclosure wall by the western gate.

15. The path soon leaves the open moor and runs between stone walls on the edge of the reservoir plantation as it descends towards Burrator Lake. Take the left fork when it divides at an open area ¼ mile after reaching the trees and again just before Norsworthy Bridge.

WALK 20C

16. Follow Walk 20B to Crazywell Cross (12). Turn left (N) here walking uphill back to the leat. Turn right along the leat but don't cross it, the easier path being on the near bank.
17. Follow the leat for 1 mile to **Older Bridge** (*5982 7055*) where it is crossed by a stony track (this will be your return route). Cross the bridge and continue beside the leat for 0.6 miles as it bends around the hillside, passing a small waterworks building known as **Drivage Hut**, then a sluice which sometimes feeds the Meavy.
18. A short distance from the sluice to the left of the leat is **Hutchinson's Cross** (*5995 6991*).

Much more modern than most of Dartmoor's crosses, Hutchinson's Cross is cut from a single piece of granite and stands in large boulder, occupying the socket of an ancient cross that once stood here. The current cross was erected in 1968 by Lt. Commander B. Hutchinson R.N. as a memorial to his mother Mrs S.L. Hutchinson. The shaft bears the inscription 'S.L.H' on the western face and '1887 – 1966' on the eastern.

19. ~200 yards beyond the cross the leat enters a short gorge and disappears into a **tunnel**.

For most of its length the Devonport Leat makes a series of loops as it gently descends from the high moor. Hence whilst a straight line from its

Nun's Cross & Farm

start on the West Dart to entering Burrator Lake measures 6½ miles the leat's meandering route following contours around the sides of hills covers more than 15 miles. The 18th century engineers however had to negotiate two areas where the topography was more challenging. Raddick Hill and crossing the River Meavy were overcome with the waterfall and aqueduct but another solution was needed to take the leat from the Dart watershed at head of the Swincombe Valley into the upper Meavy Valley. The answer was a stone-lined tunnel that runs for 640 yards under the hill. The current tunnel was constructed with the help of tinners around 1850, replacing the original that linked several existing adits (horizontal passages) from Nun's Cross Mine.

20. Take a narrow path that rises left from the leat just before it enters the gorge and tunnel. Immediately on the left is the ruin of **Old Farm** (***6016 6990***).

The ruin standing beneath a beech tree was known by former residents of Nun's Cross Farm as 'Old Farm' but its origin is unclear. It is larger than tinners' huts and some sources say it was a small farm but others that it was built as a smithy for workers constructing the leat, then used by miners.

21. The path runs through workings of **Nun's Cross Tin Mine**, passing discarded stones from their streaming and reaches **Nun's Cross** (***6048 6995***) after ¼ mile.

Standing over 7 feet high, Nun's Cross is perhaps the most impressive of all Dartmoor's crosses and is certainly one of the most ancient, dating from either Saxon or early medieval times. It was originally known as Siward's Cross, possibly referring to Siward, the Saxon Earl of Northumberland, who owned large areas of land around Tavistock prior to the Norman Conquest. The word 'SIWARD' is engraved on the eastern face. On the western face is engraved 'BOC LOND' referring to its role as marking the boundary between the Manor of Walkhampton to the west and the Forest of Dartmoor to the east. The former was owned by Buckland Abbey whose name may be a corruption of 'Book Land' meaning land owned under a charter and the inscription on the cross appears to be intended to record this.

The derivation of the name Nun's Cross is unknown and there seems to be no connection with nuns, either actual or legendary. Hence there is no consistency as to whether it is written with an apostrophe and if so where it is placed. It has been suggested that 'nuns' is a corruption of 'nans', an ancient Celtic word meaning valley, the cross standing at the head of the River Swincombe. Dartmoor has many crosses and whilst none are alike, Nun's Cross is remarkable not only for its age but also for its unusual appearance. Both arms are short, especially for its great height, and one deeper than the other, giving a slightly lopsided appearance. The shaft was broken and repaired in 1846 when two lads pushed it over.

22. Just beyond the cross is **Nun's Cross Farm**.

It is hard to imagine why John Cooper chose to build his farmhouse on this remote spot. He wasn't a Dartmoor man but saw potential to make a living here, leased a smallholding from the Duchy of Cornwall and built enclosures and a house overlooking Fox Tor Mire, moving in with his wife in 1871. After buying a cow his limited funds had virtually disappeared but over time he made a success of the venture, bringing up a family here and eventually selling a £100 worth of cattle each year. Probably the most isolated dwelling remaining on the moor, Nun's Cross Farm is now owned by an adventure company and used as a bunk house sleeping up to 36 people. There is no electricity and visitors are directed to the leat for water.

23. Return to Nun's Cross then take the hard track in the opposite

direction to the farm (NNE). This well-maintained track is one of Dartmoor's designated mountain bike routes.
24. Three **boundary stones** marked 'PCWW 1917' are passed. These mark the boundary of the catchment area for Burrator Reservoir. Smaller stones stand close to the 1st and 3rd PCWW stones. These may mark the boundary of the parishes of Dartmoor Forest (formerly Lydford) and Walkhampton. The second has a hole in it so may once have been a gatepost.
25. After 0.6 miles a crossroads with another stony track is reached (**6020 7085**). There is a fourth **PCWW stone** here. A car park on the Princetown – Whiteworks road 200 yards on the right, makes this a possible alternative start / finish point for the walk.
26. Turn left onto the track returning to the Devonport Leat again at Older Bridge after 0.3 miles. Continue on what is known as the **Monks' Path**.

Marked by crosses at intervals across the moor, the Monks' Path was once a route linking Buckfast and Tavistock Abbeys. Some parts are still clear paths whilst others are just a route across open moor. The section covered by this walk was also known as the Peat Cot Track and was the only track to this remote hamlet prior to construction of the road from Princetown. As it predated both the Devonport Leat and most tin mining, it is likely that the exact route has changed over the years. Whether it actually was used by monks is of course a matter of conjecture.

27. After ½ mile **Newleycombe Cross** (**5919 7031**) is passed on the left, from where there is a good view of Burrator Lake and its surrounding tors.

Crosses come thick and fast on this part of the moor, but whilst they may have helped travelling monks, in many cases consecutive crosses are not visible from each other, so knowledge of the route is required. One hopes that monks were familiar with the moor but in bad weather it cannot have been an easy journey.

28. Crazywell Cross soon appears on the skyline but disappears from view where its path diverges to the right. Stay on the main path which is followed for 1¼ miles back to Norsworthy Bridge, passing **Crazy Well Farm** - as Walk 20B (14).

WALK 21

EXPLORING MERRIVALE : 1½ MILES *

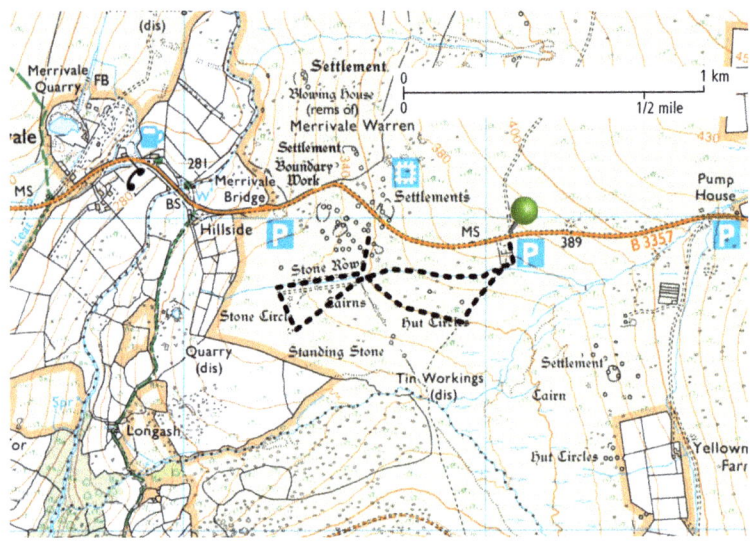

An easy, short and almost level walk exploring one of the most impressive collection of archaeological remains on Dartmoor, plus various more recent items of interest. The remains are close to the road but many drive by oblivious to the antiquities nearby. The walk starts at a car park with its own interesting history.

Start – Four Winds car park on B3357 Tavistock to Princetown road (**561 749**), 1 mile W of Princetown junction at Rundlestone. The car park is easily recognised as behind it is a walled area surrounded by trees, which was once a moorland school.

Walkhampton Foggintor School opened in 1915 to educate children from nearby cottages occupied by quarry workers. The substantial building was centrally heated and children would use the pipes for warming their pasties. It had two classrooms and there were initially

55 pupils, but numbers dwindled as quarrying declined and the school closed in 1936. It only ever had one head teacher, Fred Stoyle, who was the youngest in the country. The school was demolished in 1964 and the adjacent house which accommodated the teachers, a year later. The large fir tree still standing behind the car park dates back to the school but there are two stories as to its origin. According to Fred Stoyle, it was the family's Christmas tree which his son Ivan planted in the school garden in 1924, whilst Eric Green from Princetown, a former pupil, recalled that it was a gift from quarrymen to the school in its final year of operation.

1. Walk through the walled area (a **sheep creep** can be seen in the wall on the right) and exit at the back through a **pinch stile**, a V shaped gap in the wall designed to allow people but not sheep to pass through, immediately reaching **Longash Leat**.

Starting from a stream just to the east, the leat was built to provide water to cottages at the bottom of Longash Hill. It was cut in the 1880s, with granite slabs along the sides added later to prevent leakage and still acts as a water supply.

2. Cross the leat on a single-slab **clapper bridge**, turn right and follow it towards the Merrivale antiquities. Divert around patches

Merrivale Stone Row & Cist

Kistvaen

of reeds and mud if required. A second **clapper bridge** is soon passed. This was modified in 2021 to allow access for mobility scooters to this part of the moor.

3. On the opposite side of the leat, ~90 yards beyond the 2nd clapper, is a rectangular **dressed block of granite**, a relic from the extensive quarrying in this area.
4. As you walk a view opens up right to the tiny settlement of Merrivale and the remains of its quarry, which closed in 1997. To the left is King's Tor, with the old Princetown railway skirting the hill (Walk 23).
5. After ~⅓ mile the leat reaches two **double stone rows** which run either side of it.

The northern row is about 200 yards long and the southern one 300 yards. Like all Dartmoor's stone rows, their purpose is a mystery. Both run roughly east to west but are not entirely parallel and neither align with a significant sunrise or sunset. They do align with the rising in mid-May of the Pleiades, a group of stars also known as the Seven Sisters, which were used in ancient times to predict harvesting times, but whether this is significant is unknown.

6. Follow the row on the left for ~80 yards where an impressive **kistvaen** can be found just to the left.

One of Dartmoor's largest cists, the granite chest was excavated in 1895, when a flint knife, scraper and whetstone (sharpening implement) were found. Unfortunately the large capstone was split in the 1870s and the central piece used to make two gateposts.

Apple Crusher

7. Take a path diagonally left (approx. SE) that curves from the cist towards a **standing stone**. Just before this is **Merrivale Stone Circle (*5533 7464*)**.

Consisting of 11 fairly small stones, Merrivale's well-preserved stone circle was excavated in the late 18th century. Nothing of interest was found within the circle but a series of pits nearby suggested that there may once have been larger stones outside. A single stone 9 metres to the south east of the circle may have been an outlier that was used in astronomical sightings. The impressive menhir nearby is 10 feet (3 metres) tall.

8. Turn right (N) at the menhir, passing the stone circle and reaching the double terminal stones of the southern stone row after ~200 yards. Follow the row, passing a **kistvaen** inside a retaining circle. This feature within a stone row is most unusual.

9. On reaching the terminal stone at the end of the stone row, cross to the end of the northern row and continue N on a vague path towards the road, walking in the direction of Roos Tor, the 3rd on the right on the ridge above Merrivale Quarry. Two **hut circles** are soon passed. At the second (larger) of these head diagonally right (NE : direction of Great Mis Tor, the large tor to

the right of the valley ahead) towards a fallen wall. A further **hut circle** is passed then just beyond the wall is a rounded stone, probably an abandoned medieval **apple crusher** (*5551 7494*).

The rounded granite slab is generally considered to be an apple crusher, although it has also been suggested that it is an abandoned top stone for a crazing mill used for grinding tin ore. There are many references to food being left at Merrivale during the plague, to be picked up later by locals who left money in exchange. Most say it was left on the stone rows but it is also said that the apple crusher was used and known as the Plague Stone.

10. Return to the stone rows and from the terminal stone of the southern row take a path diagonally right (~SE : direction of Yellowmeade Farm ahead) towards a **standing stone** which is reached after ~130 yards.

Incised with a 'T' on one side (Tavistock) and an 'A' on the other (Ashburton), the stone is one of a number marking an ancient pack horse route between the towns. They date from the late 17th or early 18th century and were erected following an Act of Parliament in 1696 that empowered Justices to erect guide stones assisting travellers following tracks across the moor.

11. Continue straight on, soon reaching another **T-A stone**, this one broader and shorter than the last. It was re-erected by the DPA in 1984.

12. The path continues towards a third **T-A stone**, but half way to this divert ~50 yards left to see an intriguing arrangement of two rocks, one placed upon the other, with smaller stones wedging them apart. The top one would have been wedged in this position to be worked by a stonemason but for some reason was abandoned before the work was started.

13. Return to the path and continue to the next **T-A stone** which is surrounded by granite boulders and thinner than the previous two.

14. 35 yards beyond the third T-A stone is a rectangular **dressed block of granite**, another relic from quarrying times. From here turn left, returning to Four Winds.

WALK 22

TAVY CLEAVE & RATTLE BROOK

WALK 22A : LOWER TAVY CLEAVE : 2¼ / 3¼ MILES **

WALK 22B : TAVY CLEAVE, RATTLE BROOK, WHEAL GEORGE WHEEL PIT, HARE & GER TORS : 5 MILES ****

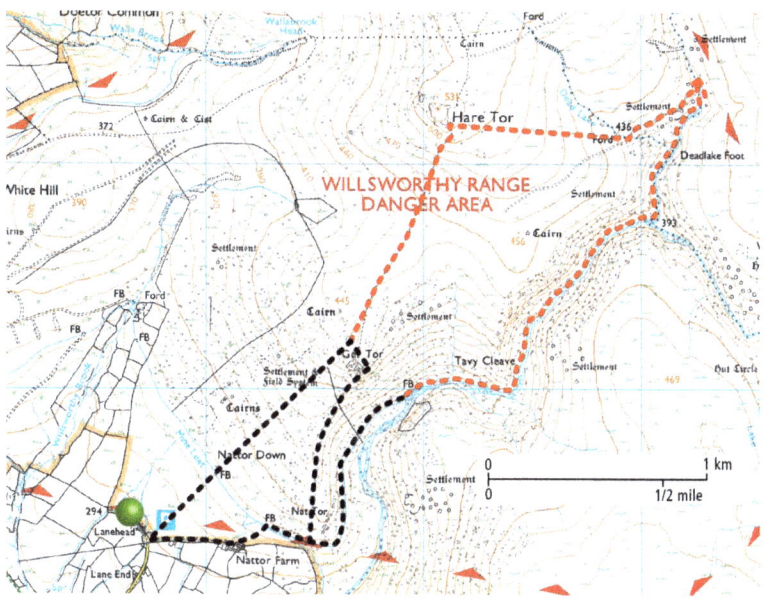

Walk 22A – A walk on paths to the bottom of Dartmoor's most spectacular moorland gorge, with the option to climb a tor and view the cleave from above.

Walk 22B continues through the gorge and completes a circuit visiting a boundary stone and the abandoned wheelpit of a tin mine in the remote Rattle Brook Valley, before returning over Hare Tor & Ger Tor with spectacular views in all directions. Paths are intermittent in some sections and some ground is rough.

Warnings:

Both walks are within the Willsworthy Firing Range.

There are some drops from the narrow path alongside the leat and adjacent fast running water.

Walk 22B - Walking through the cleave is not for the faint hearted. The path is patchy, there are boggy areas to negotiate and many large boulders to clamber over.

Start – Lane End (**537 824**). Small car park at the end of the lane from Mary Tavy through Horndon & Willsworthy.

Walk 22A

1. Follow the stony track alongside a wall for ¼ mile to Nattor Farm, then bend left on an ascending grassy path, reaching a bridge over the **Wheal Friendship Leat** after ~200 yards.

Also known as Mine Leat, this was constructed in the early part of the 19th century to provide power to Wheel Friendship Mine in Mary Tavy, which extended under the streets of the village. Water wheels drove the crushers and huge pumps that prevented the mine flooding. Access to this low cost source of energy was one of the main reasons why the mine was successful, competitors having to use coal or peat to power steam turbines. Copper, arsenic, lead and iron were all mined here. Although mining ceased in 1925 the leat remains in use, serving Mary Tavy hydro-electric power station and producing green energy from Dartmoor. Once the largest hydro-electric plant in England, Mary Tavy still generates enough power to supply 1,700 homes, Number One Plant being driven by water from the River Tavy and Number Two Plant by the Wheel Friendship Leat.

2. Turn right, following the narrow path on the right bank of the fast-flowing leat. This soon passes a concrete bridge below Nat Tor, then bends sharp left as it enters the valley of the River Tavy, giving your first view of the cleave ahead. After ¾ mile the leat

View to Tavy Cleave from Ger Tor

meets the river (**5495 8299**) where a small stone building stands beside a low weir.

3. There are three stone bridges but if the level is high the leat can overflow as a torrent back into the Tavy, so then only the first crossing can be used. Walk 22B continues up the cleave.
4. For Walk 22A return along the leat to the concrete bridge below Nat Tor, just after a sharp bend right. Options are now to return by the outward route or cross the leat and take a vague path roughly N to **Ger Tor** for fine views of Tavy Cleave. Approach the tor from the left side. On the tor is a military **flag pole** and an **observation hut** (on the river side of the tor, with the entrance on the S side – take care as steep slope below).

The observation or range hut is one of a number which were built by the army on high ground on Northern Dartmoor and used by range wardens to prevent walkers wandering into live firing areas. Most of the original stone huts have been replaced by metal huts which are delivered by helicopter. This one remains and is well concealed, being built into a wall, but is no longer used by the military.

5. Pick up the path from Hare Tor, ~175 yards NW of Ger Tor, which descends to the leat, crosses on a bridge and continues to Lane End car park.

Walk 22B

6. Follow Walk 22A to the leat intake (3). The next mile is one of the most spectacular walks on Dartmoor but the path is intermittent and you will need to climb over large boulders.
7. Cross the leat and climb a steep path immediately on the left after the hut. This avoids the boggy area close to the water. Follow the rough path as it returns closer to the river, heading upstream.

The steep gorge of Tavy Cleave is not typical Dartmoor but is one of the most majestic and beautiful places in the National Park. You will pass small waterfalls splashing over rocks into pools which are easily deep enough for swimming, although there may be strong undercurrents so much care is needed. It is a truly wonderful place and there are many spots to sit and enjoy the beauty.

8. The river bends sharp left and the gorge soon narrows. Soon after the left bend a large pool with a low waterfall above it is reached. This is the **Devil's Kitchen** (*5545 8312*), a most picturesque spot.
9. A mile from the leat intake the Tavy bends right but before this the path all but disappears and very involved boulder hopping is required. Turn back if you do not feel confident to negotiate this.

Wheel Friendship Leat Looking to Tavy Cleave

Willsworthy Boundary Stone & Deadlake

On the bend the Tavy is joined by the Rattle Brook. Two miles of hard walking ahead is Fur Tor, Dartmoor's most remote tor, but our walk follows the Rattle Brook then the Hare Tor / Ger Tor ridge.

10. Turn left along the Rattle Brook where there is a path of sorts but keep well above the river to avoid mires. After ¼ mile Dead Lake, a small tributary of the Rattle Brook, is reached. This enters the Rattle Brook at **Deadlake Foot** by a ford, alongside which is a **Willsworthy Boundary Stone** (*5613 8404*).

Engraved 'WD 21', this is one of 46 boundary stones erected in the early 1900s to mark out the Willsworthy firing range. These mainly followed the line of Willsworthy Manor, 3,448 acres of which were purchased by the War Office for military training.

11. Cross Dead Lake and continue on a patchy path ~100 yards above the Rattle Brook for a further ¼ mile to the point where it's crossed by a track at another ford (*5626 8837*).

12. Cross the stream at the ford and walk right for ~120 yards to the ruin of a mining **wheel pit** (*5631 8427*).

Built for the small Wheal George tin mine in the 1850s, the 2 metre high walls would have contained a water powered wheel. The adjacent platform was the dressing floor where ore was sorted and washed, however the absence of a completed leat to supply water suggests that this may not have actually been used.

13. Re-cross the stream at the ford and continue on the track (SSE) soon passing a Bronze Age **hut circle**. This is part of a significant complex of settlements on either side of the Rattle Brook.

14. Stay on the patchy track for ~⅓ mile. **Hare Tor** can be seen to the right (although after a while it falls from view), however this is most easily reached not directly but by heading to a point ~200 yards above Deadlake Foot. From here is a wonderful view up the Tavy to Fur Tor. Cross Dead Lake at a ford and follow an initially stony then grassy path that soon bends right and climbs 0.6 miles to the tor.

Hare Tor affords superb views in all directions. Looking into the moor, ahead are Amicombe Hill, the Tavy Valley and Fur Tor in the centre of Dartmoor. Tavy Cleave Tors and Ger Tor are to the right and to the west Bodmin Moor can be seen in the distance. There is a military flag pole on the tor.

15. From the left (S) side of Hare Tor follow a path for ¾ mile to Ger Tor. Note that this is not the path that heads south to rocks above the river which are not named on the OS Map but marked as Tavy Cleave Tors on the British Mountain Map. **Ger Tor** is to the right of these.

16. The view from Ger Tor gives another perspective of Tavy Cleave as the river winds through the steep sided rocky valley. See 4 for details of **observation hut**.

17. Return to the path from Hare Tor (~175 yards from Ger Tor) which descends to the leat, crosses on a bridge and continues to Lane End car park.

Ger Tor Observation Hut

WALK 23

PRINCETOWN RAILWAY & QUARRIES

23A – PRINCETOWN RAILWAY & FOGGINTOR QUARRY: 4 MILES *

23B – CONTINUES TO SWELL TOR & INGRA TOR QUARRIES: 8 MILES *

BOTH WALKS *** IF YOU CHOOSE TO ENTER THE QUARRIES.

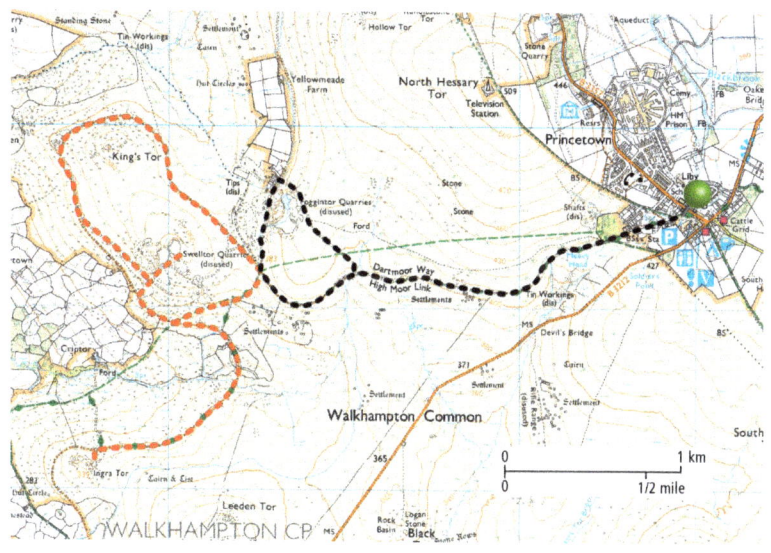

Walk 23A - An easy walk on good paths to the picturesque Foggintor Quarry, following a railway line across the moor which closed more than sixty years ago.

Walk 23B continues to the historic Swell Tor Quarry, then on to Ingra Tor Quarry and the sites of two of our remotest railway stations.

Warning:

Great care should be taken around the quarries, particularly Foggintor where there are unfenced sudden drops and deep water.

Start – Main car park in the centre of Princetown (**589 735**). Charged. Toilets. This is adjacent to the National Park Information Centre in the old Duchy Hotel.

Walk 23A

1. Turn left from the car park entrance, following a lane for a short distance past the fire station, to a path (left) by the site of the old **Princetown railway station**, signed 'Princetown Railway'.

The station master's house and railway cottages still stand on the right but all that remains of the station is a GWR stable building by the path. This dates from around 1909 and housed the horses that hauled carts around the town carrying goods arriving by train.

2. Pass through a gate and follow the path, initially between fences, then onto the **railway line** as it makes its way across the moor.

The railway from Yelverton to Princetown opened in 1883, much of its traffic being prisoners, officers and supplies to Dartmoor Prison, as well as serving quarries, locals and walkers. The line closed in 1956 but the moorland track bed survives and is an excellent walking and cycle route.

3. After ¾ mile the line passes through a cutting above which are **boundary stones** on each side.

Their inscription PCWW 1917 denotes Plymouth Corporation Water Works and the year the stones were erected. They are two of a series of posts marking the 13 mile boundary of the water catchment area for Burrator Reservoir.

4. A bridge is reached after a further ~100 yards (**5705 7318**). Leave the railway to the right just before the bridge, descend to a small stream and cross this, then take a path which soon bears diagonally left (NW) up the hill.

5. The edge of **Foggintor Quarry** is soon reached and great care should be taken here, especially in poor visibility or if the ground

Foggintor Quarry

is slippery. There are unfenced drops to the quarry and a fall would be fatal. Bear right above the quarry until dropping down to the main entrance close to some ruined buildings.

Foggintor Quarry was active from around 1820 to 1938 and supplied the granite for Nelson's Column, as well as Princetown Prison. Up to 400 people once worked here and the remains of their houses and offices can still be seen, although some of the stones were used in the building of nearby North Hessary Tor television mast. The ruined walls that still stand were once the quarry master's house and the remains of a sunken kitchen garden can be seen nearby. The arch beneath the house was a dynamite store.

As one would expect, this beautiful but mysterious place holds its own Dartmoor legend, however this one turned out to be true. Tales of strange grey figures known as 'shadow men' lurking in the quarry at night seemed to be just another of the moor's myths but after some decades the truth was revealed. The grey men were elite soldiers on top secret training missions. The quarry is still used for military training and

Site of King Tor Halt

it's not unusual to see marines abseiling down the rocks. Spikes for fixing ropes can be seen above the quarry.

6. There is a path through the quarry which can be followed with care but it starts with quite a drop over a large rock and may be boggy by the exit. Alternatively follow the track left (S) from by the ruined buildings. Both routes rejoin the railway line after ~⅓ mile at the site of **King Tor Halt** (*5652 7321*).

One of the most remote stations in England, King Tor Halt was only open for 28 years and once the quarries closed in the 1930s its few passengers were walkers. The wooden platform is long gone and just the concrete base of a shelter remains. The station was named after the nearby tor, although that is King's rather than King.

The track heads off towards King's Tor, however the next station was at Ingra Tor, which can be seen a mile ahead and in the opposite direction. The line rounds King's Tor then reappears a few hundred yards below the halt, having completed a loop of 1¼ miles. A further loop around the side of the valley requires another mile to reach Ingra Tor Halt, meaning that in order for the railway to gain height at a workable gradient the distance between the halts is 3½ times greater than the direct route. There are various tales of passengers racing the train between the

Swell Tor Corbels

two halts. King Tor & Ingra Tor halts feature in a chapter of my book **Remote Stations**.

7. Walk 23B leaves here. For Walk 23A turn left along the railway, reaching the bridge where you left it after ~½ mile, then continuing back to Princetown.

Walk 23B

8. Follow Walk 23A to (7). Turn right along the railway track, following it around King's Tor. There are excellent views of the moor, to Plymouth Sound and into Cornwall. Merrivale Quarry and some of the Merrivale Bronze Age remains (Walk 21) can be seen to the right.

9. 1 mile from King Tor Halt the railway crosses a (fenced) bridge then runs along an embankment. At the end of the embankment (**5544 7365**) a branch to **Swell Tor Quarry** leaves on the left. Follow this grassy track for ½ mile to the entrance to the quarry, soon (¼ mile) passing abandoned **bridge corbels**.

Wooden sleepers can still be seen on the trackbed of the quarry branch and beside it are 12 corbels that were cut for use in widening the old London Bridge in 1903. These were either seconds or surplus to requirements and were never collected, so have lain on the moor for over a century. In 1967 the bridge was purchased by an American businessman and shipped to Arizona but sustained some damage on the way and it is said that unused corbels were sent from Dartmoor as replacements, although I have been unable to substantiate the story.

10. The quarry is best entered (with care) by a narrow path on the bank to the left of the entrance, as ground level is very wet.

Close to the entrance to the quarry are the remains of several stone buildings, one of which was a blacksmith's workshop, and a stone platform from which trucks were loaded. Granite from here was used in the construction of the Thames Embankment. The cavernous quarry cut out of the hillside is an atmospheric and awe inspiring sight. Now reclaimed by nature, it is a place of beauty, with trees perched on tiny ledges on the granite faces.

11. After exploring the quarry walk downhill to the right of spoil heaps to rejoin the main Princetown Railway track and turn left along this.
12. After ⅓ mile a path leaves to the left, a short cut back to King Tor Halt. This will be your return route.
13. Continue on the railway as it bends sharp right and passes under a **stone bridge** which was built to allow livestock to cross the railway. ½ mile beyond this are **Ingra Tor Halt (5557 7222)** & **Quarry**. The quarry is to your left and the site of the station to the right.

Little remains of Ingra Tor Halt, which was once famous for a sign on the platform warning of snakes. The concrete base of a wooden hut on a raised bank and a few bits of wood by the trackbed are its only remnants. The wooden platform is long gone. The station was built in 1937 when granite waste from the quarry was taken away for road dressing but then kept until the line closed to serve walkers. My father used the station in 1955 and his reminiscences are included in **Remote Stations**. *Ingra Tor Quarry is smaller than Foggintor & Swell Tor but is notable for two stone circular crane supports which remain on the ground.*

14. Return along the railway then shortly before Swell Tor Quarry take the path uphill on the right (**5629 7286**) which is a short cut to King Tor Halt. Turn right where this rejoins the railway and return to Princetown.

WALK 24

CONCHIE ROAD & CROCK OF GOLD : 3¾ MILES *

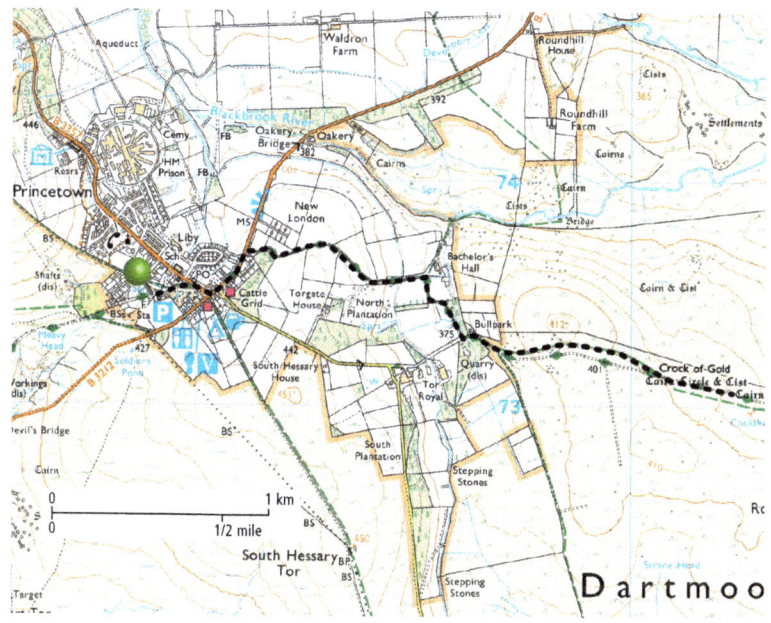

An easy and fairly level walk on paths to a Bronze Age burial chamber, following the historic 'road to nowhere'.

Start – Main car park in the centre of Princetown (**589 735**). Charged. Toilets.

Princetown was established in the late 1700s by Sir Thomas Tyrwhitt, with the aim to farm the moorland that surrounds it. He was responsible for the famous prison which was constructed in 1809 to hold Napoleonic prisoners of war. The imposing buildings that dominate the town once held up to 6,000 men and whilst they are still in use for much smaller numbers, its days as an operational prison are numbered.

1. Turn right from the car park, passing the **National Park**

Information Centre in the old Duchy Hotel, which is well worth visiting.

2. At the crossroads turn left. Cross the road and soon pass a drinking **water fountain** by a small green. This was a gift of by R.H. Hooke Esq in grateful acknowledgment for '*the life-giving air of Princetown*'.

3. Just after Oakery Crescent and before Sunnyside house, take a bridleway passing through a gate on the right. A strange **metal contraption** is seen after a few yards.

Former Dousland Crossing Gate

The rusting metal was once the mechanism for the level crossing gates on the Princetown railway at Dousland. Redundant for their original purpose when the line closed in 1956, the gates were bought by the tenant of what was then Sunnyside Farm and used as a cattle crush.

4. Follow the path as it bends left and right around a small wood, then a line of trees, climbing gently onto open moor and revealing a wide panorama of Northern Dartmoor. Four old **gateposts** with ironwork are passed between here and the next track.

5. The path descends, crossing the **Devonport Leat** (*5993 7356*) (Walk 20) and soon reaching a hard track. Just before this is a mysterious stone construction of two parallel walls. I have been unable to determine the origin or use of this. It is too wide for a cattle crush and may once have had a roof and been used for farming purposes.

6. Turn right onto the track signed 'Peat Cot'. To the left is **Bachelor's Hall**.

Bachelor's Hall was built as a corn mill and bakery in the late 18th century but has seen use as a naptha works for distilling peat, tin smelting works and farm. The last farmer left in 1944 and after being empty for many years it is now a camping barn.

7. Follow the track for ~¼ mile, passing through two gates, then when it meets a concrete roadway turn left, immediately passing **Bull Park**.

Bull Park Farm was built by Sir Thomas Tyrwhitt for a cattle herdsman, with enclosures to separate bulls from cows and calves. The last tenant farmer left in 1957, after which the house became a holiday cottage but is now a private home.

8. A gate just beyond the house leads to Royal Hill by the '**Conchie Road**'.

In WW1 Dartmoor Prison was used to house more than 1,000 conscientious objectors, who for religious or political reasons had refused to join the military after conscription was introduced in 1916. They were required to carry out work of national importance and were working on a plan to develop the land around Princetown for agriculture, for which a road was required to link farms. The 'Conchies' as they became known, constructed a road across Royal Hill but the war ended before it could be completed. With the land too poor to cultivate the route was of little use and became known as 'The Road to Nowhere', or the

Crock of Gold

'Conchie Road'. In November 2018, following a vigil held outside the Dartmoor Information Centre, a small plaque was unveiled to honour the conscientious objectors who had toiled on the moor building a road that goes nowhere. The plaque can be seen on the left gatepost.

9. Follow the Conchie Road, which bears left when the track divides after ~120 yards. After a further ~575 yards another track is passed on the right. This also goes nowhere, coming to an end on the slopes of Royal Hill.

10. ~600 yards beyond this track there is a mound of stone and earth to the left of the track. A short distance to the right is the **Crock of Gold (*6128 7306*)**. Note that some maps wrongly show it on the left of the track.

The moor around Royal Hill was a popular burial area for Bronze Age people and there are at least ten kistvaens in the area. Although the well-formed rectangular tomb is fairly small (but deep) and probably contained a cremation rather than burial, the Crock of Gold is the most impressive. It is surrounded by a retaining circle, although part is missing and of course has its own legend.

According to Dartmoor folklore the cist contained gold that had been buried with a chieftain, however no one dared investigate the tomb as it was believed that this would bring forth evil curses. Luke Mudge lived on the edge of Royal Hill and made a living from making nets for warreners. He had often thought of the gold buried on the moor but resisted claiming it for fear of the curses. Unfortunately one day he spilled boiling water on his hand so was unable to work and with no income his thoughts turned to the gold. On a moonlit night he took an iron bar to the cist and forced the lid open. Groping inside however he felt nothing but broken pottery, but before he could remove his hand the moon disappeared and in pitch darkness the lid slid back. Luke was trapped and could do nothing but lie in agony hoping help would arrive. By the time a passing miner found him he was close to death. With his hand now withered, after a long spell in Tavistock Hospital Luke was sent to the workhouse, his plight a lesson that the ghosts of the ancient deceased will not allow anyone to disturb their graves.

11. Return to Princetown by the outward route.

WALK 25

NUN'S CROSS FARM, FOX TOR & DUCKS' POOL

WALK 25A: CHILDE'S TOMB, FOX TOR, NUN'S CROSS FARM & CROSS : 4½ MILES **

WALK 25B: CONTINUES TO BLACK LANE, DUCKS' POOL & PHILLPOTTS' CAVE : 8½ MILES ****

WALK 25C: CIRCULAR WALK TO NUN'S CROSS FARM & CROSS : 2 MILES *

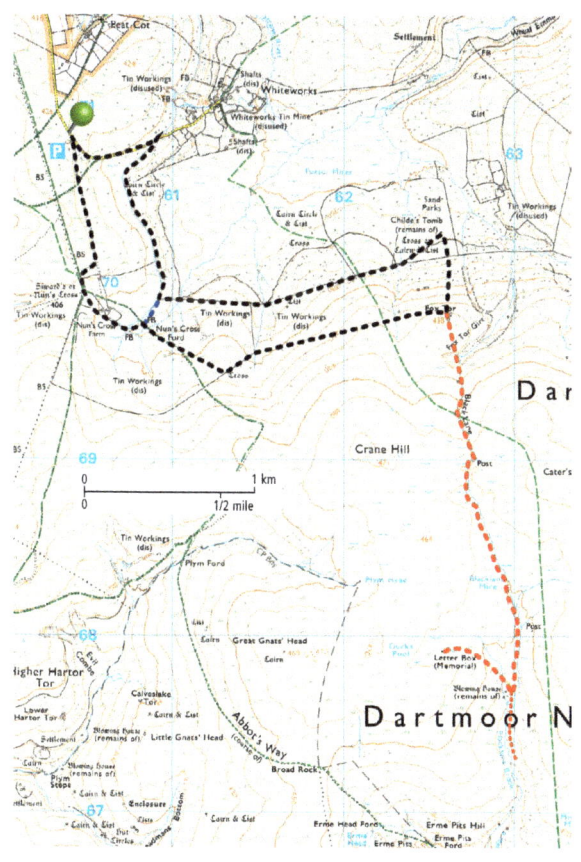

Walk 25A - A walk mostly on paths, some of which are rough, around the edge of Dartmoor's famous Fox Tor Mire, to a legendary monument, returning past a remote farm and possibly the moor's oldest cross.

Walk 25B continues along an ancient route into the centre of Southern Dartmoor, visiting a legendary cave and one of the moor's iconic letterboxes.

Walk 25C is a short circular route on paths with fine views across wild Dartmoor, following the start and end of Walk 25A.

Warnings:

Do not be tempted to take a short cut across Fox Tor Mire.

Walk 8B enters into the wild and featureless centre of Southern Dartmoor. It is very easy to get lost here. Anyone undertaking this walk must be suitably equipped and competent in the use of map & compass. Some of the ground is very boggy, especially after wet weather, but at any time of the year one can expect to get wet feet.

Start – Car park (**6038 7079**) on right on the continuation of Tor Royal Lane from Princetown to Whiteworks, just before the lane turns sharp left towards the end of the road, 2 miles from Princetown. This is the third and largest of 3 car parks on the right of the lane and is set back slightly from the road. A track leaves from the left (S) of the car park entrance and this will be your return route.

Walk 25A

1. Follow the lane as it bends sharp left, soon revealing an impressive view across wild Dartmoor. Fox Tor can be seen in the distance but do not contemplate walking directly to the tor as the depression between it and you is **Fox Tor Mire**.

The most notorious of Dartmoor's bogs, Fox Tor Mire was the inspiration for Sir Arthur Conan Doyle's Grimpen Mire, haunt of the terrifying beast in Hound of the Baskervilles. Maps show a path across the mire, which does not exist, however it can be crossed (I have done so myself) but only with great care. I would strongly recommend following the route I describe and not venturing into the mire. It can be highly dangerous even if one of its legends may be an exaggeration.

A young man was walking across the moor when he spied a splendid top hat. Stopping to pick it up he was somewhat shocked to find that beneath it was a man's head. The gentleman smiled and introduced himself but was stuck fast in the mire. The walker tugged but could not extricate the man. Again he smiled and suggested that if the young man would wait a moment he would take his feet out of the stirrups of the horse that he was sat upon.

2. After ⅓ mile the lane crosses a bridge over the **Devonport Leat** (**6089 7082**)(Walk 20). Turn right following the left bank of the attractive leat as it gently descends across the moor. A metal **girder bridge** is soon passed. On a bend just before a wall is a **sheep leap** (**6069 7061**). Looking back the tiny settlement of **Whiteworks** can be seen at the end of the lane.

Whiteworks was once one of Dartmoor's largest tin mines with two waterwheels to crush ore and pump out shafts. Three workers' cottages still stand and other remains including flooded shafts can be seen, some being fenced off for safety. Mining here was most active in the 19th century but finally ceased in 1914, when farming took over.

3. After ⅔ mile, soon after passing a second **girder bridge**, a drystone wall meets the left bank of the leat (**6091 6990**). This spot is known as **Sunny Corner**. Turn left here, following a grassy path to the left of the wall. This descends and soon crosses the infant River Swincombe which passes through a gap under the wall.

4. Continue on the undulating path left of the wall, crossing three more streams each in their own dip where ground may be boggy. Descending to the last of these, which is in a rocky area, Fox Tor can be seen on the hill to the right. In the distance is Ter Hill, on

Childe's Tomb

the slopes of which can be seen the remains of **Fox Tor Farm**, a setting for Eden Phillpotts' **American Prisoner.**

5. A few yards beyond the final stream the path divides. Take the left fork (initially very narrow) diagonally away from the wall, reaching **Childe's Tomb** (**6257 7028**) after ~175 yards.

Childe's Tomb may be based on a kistvaen, although most of the structure is relatively recent. According to legend, the cross, which stands on a substantial base of granite blocks, marks the spot where Amyas Childe of Plymstock, known as Childe the Hunter, died in the 14th century. In stormy weather Childe became separated from his hunting companions and lost on the moors, realised he was in danger of freezing to death. In an attempt to keep warm he killed his horse, disembowelled it and crawled inside. This was however to no avail and he died from the cold but not before writing a note in blood leaving his estate of Plymstock to whichever church buried his body. The legend however did not end here, as a battle to claim his body ensued. It was found by men (possibly monks) from Tavistock but as they carried it to the abbey news reached them of a plot by residents of Plymstock to ambush them at a bridge over the Tavy. Thwarting the ambush, the monks quickly erected a new bridge outside Tavistock and smuggled Childe into the abbey, which then inherited his lands.

The monument was largely destroyed in 1812 when its stones were used in the building of Fox Tor farmhouse. It was repaired in the 1880s by Mr Fearnley Tanner and the DPA, who recovered 9 of the original 12 blocks forming the pedestal and had a new cross made in Holne.

6. Turn right at Childe's Tomb, following a path through a gateway in the wall (**6266 7016**), then ascend **Fox Tor**. The path narrows then disappears but it is not a difficult nor particularly steep climb.

The view across Fox Tor Mire to Whiteworks is one of the most atmospheric on Dartmoor but was very nearly lost in the 1970s when Plymouth Corporation and South West Devon Water Board proposed to build a 754 acre reservoir with a vast dam across the Swincombe. The reservoir and its associated infrastructure would have devastated much of Southern Dartmoor. A bill was put to Parliament and after 17 days consideration the committee of four MPs rejected it. Half a century later it seems incredible that a proposal to destroy such a wilderness would even be seriously considered, but it very nearly happened and we should be forever grateful to the campaigners who saved the moor, led by Lady Sylvia Sayer, Chair of the DPA. I should add that as Chairman of the DPA London Group, my father was present in the Westminster committee room when the announcement that the reservoir had been rejected was made on 3rd December 1970. There was much rejoicing.

7. Proceed to the furthest rocky outcrop. Walk 25B leaves here. For Walk 25A turn right (E) onto a path running along the ridge. This soon fords a stream in a gulley then passes Little Fox Tor. Nun's Cross Farm can be seen a mile ahead.

8. A granite post soon comes into view ahead (left). This is **Wheel Anne Cross** (**6132 6949**). Cross a gulley then take a path diagonally left (SE) uphill to the cross (which has now fallen out of view) reaching it after ~200 yards.

Wheel Anne Cross is also known as Whealham Bottom Cross and locally as the Armless Cross. It may originally have possessed a head with arms but now has just an incised cross.

9. Take a path right (NE) from the cross towards Nun's Cross farm, which can be seen directly ahead.

10. Just after crossing a stream the Devonport Leat is reached by a **clapper bridge** and **sluice**. Don't cross this but turn left, following the leat until just before it disappears into a **tunnel** after ~125 yards. From here a path leads to **Nun's Cross Farm** (*6059 6982*) & **Nun's Cross** (Walk 20). Walk in front of the farmhouse then through a gap in the wall (just before a tree) and through the enclosure to Nun's Cross.
11. Continue on the stony track for ~75 yards until it reaches the corner of a wall where two grassy paths diverge diagonally right. Either can be followed (the one on the right is probably preferable) as both meet the wider Nun's Cross Farm stone track. Turn left on meeting this, reaching the car park after ~⅓ mile.

Walk 25B

12. Follow Walk 25A to (7). The walk now follows an ancient route into the centre of the moor. The first objective is to find the entrance to **Black Lane**.

An ancient route across the moor, Black Lane is neither a lane nor a sunken peat pass as are found on the northern moor. It is a way between the desolate low hills of Crane Hill & Cater's Beam, linking the Swincombe Valley with the Erme and its tributaries. The route was probably made for driving cattle but is now rather wet and even the narrow paths at the edge run through boggy patches. It is marked by two railway sleepers, which are well known to Dartmoor walkers and provide invaluable guides in this wild landscape. The post at the north end is known as Cater's Beam, which is the low hill to the east. This was replaced in 2016 by Dartmoor guide and walker Richard Ware, who realised that the old one was rotting away and with the help of a local farmer erected a new sleeper. The old one was marked '69' suggesting that it had been in place for 47 years. The actual extent of Black Lane is a matter of debate. OS maps mark it as running from Fox Tor Gert to the most northerly railway sleeper, but Harvey British Mountain Map position it between the two posts.

13. Take a narrow path that runs due south from the southernmost rocks of Fox Tor, reaching the top end of Fox Tor Gert (tinning gulley) after ~200 yards.

14. Cross the gert and stream to the left of a boggy area and continue on the far side of the gert as it bends left, then switch to the right side, passing a **tinners hut** (**6266 6945**). After a while the first Black Lane marker post (**Cater's Beam**) appears in the distance.
15. Turn right at the post reaching the start of another shallow valley after a few yards. This is the Black Lane Brook or Wollake, a tributary of the River Erme. You are now crossing the watershed between the Rivers Dart and Erme. Follow patchy narrow paths (S) along the right (W) side of the valley, diverting around mires as necessary.
16. A second **railway sleeper post** is passed ~0.6 miles from the first. Do not approach this but stay on the right. An area of extensive tinning remains with stone walls is soon entered. Pass through this, bearing right, until reaching a small stream, the Ducks' Pool Stream.
17. Cross this and follow a narrow path upstream. **Ducks' Pool** (**6260 6790**) is found after ~⅓ mile on the right.

As is often the way on Dartmoor, names can be deceptive; Ducks' Pool has neither water nor ducks. It is simply a depression in the rough ground in the wilderness of central Southern Dartmoor. It is possible that the pool was drained by tinners, who were active in the area, however there is no record of it holding water. The reference to ducks may have come from its use as a more general term for waterfowl. Ducks' Pool was the site of one of Dartmoor's earliest letterboxes, where walkers traditionally sign a visitors' book and leave cards or letters to be posted by the next visitor. The letterbox was constructed in 1938 as a memorial to the Dartmoor author William Crossing.

18. Return along the stream until it meets the Black Lane Brook / Wollake. There is a **blowing house** in the angle between the two streams (**6295 6766**). Looking down the stream a rocky area can be seen ~325 yards ahead in the shallow gorge. Cross the Black Lane Brook and pick up patchy narrow paths heading for these rocks. Beneath the largest flat rock is **Phillpotts' Cave** (**6304 6729**).

Phillpotts' Cave

The cavern takes its name from the author Eden Phillpotts who wrote many books on Dartmoor. John Spencer, who worked on maintaining Black Lane, used the cave and in the early 1900s Eden Phillpotts made it slightly more homely by filling in gaps between the rocks with turf. Phillpotts stocked the cave with food and drink for the use of walkers or workers who needed to take shelter here. This started a tradition that one could always find food in the cave but that visitors should leave something for the next person to find, however in recent times the custom appears to have died out.

19. Return to Fox Tor by the outward route, crossing the stream to walk up the left side of Black Lane. Do not be tempted to walk to the first railway sleeper as it is very boggy crossing to the path from here.
20. On reaching Fox Tor follow Walk 25A from (7) to Nun's Cross Farm & back to the car park.

Walk 25C

Follow Walk 25A to (3), but rather than turning left by the wall continue beside the leat for ~160 yards to a bridge. From here pick up the instructions from Walk 25A (10) to Nun's Cross Farm & Cross and back to the car park.

WALK 26

BEARDOWN TORS & BEARDOWN MAN

WALK 26A : BEARDOWN TORS, DEVONPORT LEAT: 5 MILES **

WALK 26B : BEARDOWN TORS, WISTMAN'S WOOD: 4½ MILES **

WALK 26C : CONTINUES TO BEARDOWN MAN & BROWN'S HOUSE : 8 MILES ****

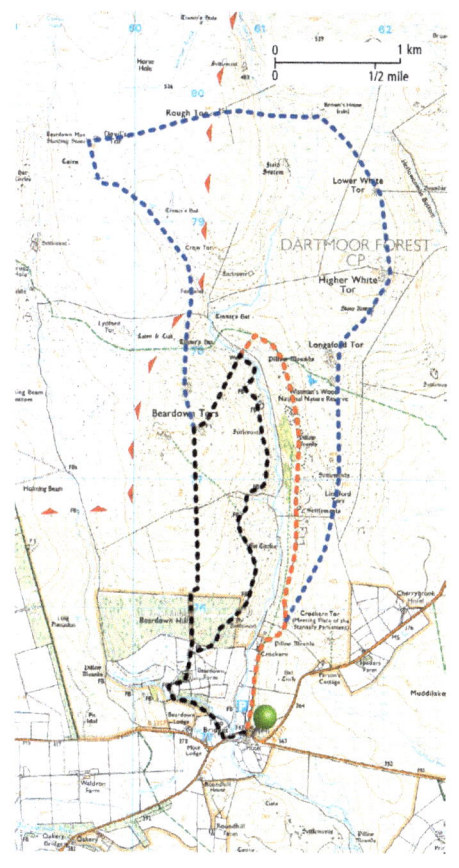

Walk 26A - A walk to an impressive tor with some of Dartmoor's best views, returning along the picturesque Devonport Leat.

Walk 26B returns past the ancient Wistman's Wood.

Walk 26C has more outstanding views as it continues on ridges either side of the West Dart, visiting the moor's most impressive single Bronze Age standing stone and the remains of possibly its most remote dwelling.

Warnings:

Walks 26A & Walk 26C cross the West Dart. Whilst this is usually fairly easy it may not be possible if the river level is high. Care is required at all times.

Much of Walk 26C is within the Merrivale Firing Range. Walks 26A & 26B do not enter the range.

With some boggy areas and rough ground towards the centre of the moor Walk 26C is best done after dry weather. Appropriate attire and navigation skills are essential if attempting this walk.

Start – Two Bridges car park (**6092 7505**) in old quarry on B3357, 1½ miles NE of Princetown. If this popular car park is full there may be space 250 yards E on the Ashburton road.

WALK 26A

1. Turn right (W) onto the road from Two Bridges car park, cross the bridge over the West Dart, then take a footpath on the right after 75 yards.
2. This crosses several stiles as it descends to the Cowsic River, then rises as a narrow path through woodland, an attractive walk above the fast flowing stream. After ⅓ mile it meets a track.
3. Turn right on the track, immediately crossing the river on the arched granite **Beardown Farm Bridge**. A small gate on the left after a few yards leads across a field to **Beardown Clapper Bridge**.

At 12 yards long Beardown Clapper is one of the most impressive on Dartmoor. After being swept away the bridge was replaced in 1793 and re-erected by the DPA following more damage in a great flood of July 1890, which also damaged the road bridge at Two Bridges.

4. Return to the gate and follow the track as it bends around Beardown Farm, soon reaching the **Devonport Leat** (Walk 20) which is crossed on a concrete bridge.
5. Continue straight on towards a conifer plantation, soon passing through a gate after which the track runs through a fire break in the trees. On leaving the plantation the track runs right then straightens to continue uphill, before petering out.
6. Continue straight (N) on along the vague path, gently climbing over easy ground to a gate in the wall ahead (**6050 7677**). This is to the right of a ladder stile.
7. Pass through the gate after which there is a track for a short distance, then a patchy path to **Beardown Tor** ahead. The tor has three main outcrops. Head for the one on the right (E) on which there is a military flagpole (**6055 7737**). Walk 26C leaves here.

From Beardown Tor there are fine views in all directions. Looking into the centre of the moor (N), to the right is the West Dart valley and the edge of Wistman's Wood. The strangely shaped Crow Tor can be seen further up the river with Rough Tor beyond it. You will visit this if following Walk 26C. Lydford Tor is closer to the left and Princetown with its prison to the south. Left (E) of Princetown is the expanse of moor visited in Walks 20 & 25 around Nun's Cross Farm & Fox Tor Mire.

8. For Walk 26A take a path running slightly right (NNE) from Beardown Tor and descending to a weir (**6085 7797**) where the Devonport Leat leaves the West Dart. **Wistman's Wood** is seen on the opposite side of the Dart.

The best known of Dartmoor's three high altitude ancient oak woods, Wistman's Wood is a remarkable and mystical place. With moss and lichens covering the stunted, twisted oaks and the granite boulders spread across the floor below, there is no doubt that wood is atmospheric; some say romantic, others that it is haunted and to be feared.

9. Cross the leat on a **clapper bridge** just below the weir. Turn right along the leat reaching the track followed outward just above Beardown Farm after 1¾ miles. Follow the outward route back to Two Bridges.

Walk 26B

10. If you wish to take a closer look at Wistman's Wood and if the Dart can be safely crossed by the weir, cross, then climb a stile over a wall. Several paths leave from here. Take the one slightly left as this avoids a boggy area to the right. Turn right on reaching a crossroads after ~275 yards. The distinctive Crow Tor can be seen to the left. Follow the path above the wood. Note that it passes through some rocky areas so walking is quite rough. *To protect the fragile habitat please do not enter Wistman's Wood. Lichens and moss which take hundreds of years to form are being destroyed by walkers, who are asked to walk around the wood.*
11. Cross a stile after the wood and continue above the river, reaching Crockern Farm where the path meets a track which is followed back to Two Bridges. The track passes a wall on the left and on the **gatepost** at the end of this can be seen the iron hanger and stone cutting marks.

WALK 26C

12. Follow Walk 26A to 7. From the south easterly outcrop of Beardown Tor take a path which runs NNW just to the left of the next part of the tor ahead.
13. From here there are several paths leading to the wall ⅓ mile ahead, which is just beyond a line of red and white poles marking the boundary of Merrivale Range. Don't take the obvious path bearing left to Lydford Tor but head to where a ladder stile crosses the wall. This is the third stile of four that you can see east of Lydford Tor. A useful guide is that just beyond the stile is a low outcrop of rocks, sometimes known as Little Lydford Tor.
14. Cross the stile and continue straight on along a patchy path to Little Lydford Tor about 250 yards ahead (***6018 7849***).

15. Go left of the rocks and follow a reasonable path (patchy in places) which bears left around the contour, avoiding a boggy area higher up the hill. (Don't descend to the stream on the right). A higher rocky outcrop (**5970 7933**) soon becomes visible and is the next objective. Although the path disappears it is an easy walk up the slope to the rocks which are sometimes known as South Devil's Tor.
16. Devil's Tor can now be seen ~350 yards ahead and is approached across reasonably easy level ground, although without a path. Immediately to the left of Devil's Tor is **Beardown Man (*5958 7961*)**.

One of Dartmoor's most impressive Bronze Age remains, Beardown Man stands 3.5 metres high and probably has at least half this length beneath the ground. This immense granite slab is the moor's tallest isolated menhir, the most remote and at 542 metres above sea level, is at the highest altitude. The stone was erected here almost 4,000 years ago but its purpose is unknown; perhaps a marker, a memorial, or religious icon. It is much wider than it is thick, so appears very different when viewed from different directions. Beyond Devil's Tor is High Dartmoor and Fur Tor can be seen directly ahead. This is wildest Dartmoor and the

Beardown Man

two mile walk between the heads of the Tavy and Dart is not as easy as it might appear.

17. From Devil's Tor the route turns right (ENE) heading for Rough Tor (**6061 7983**) ~½ mile away. You will have noticed this tor (often pronounced 'Row Tor') earlier in the walk, as with several military installations around the rock it resembles a submarine on top of the hill. There are patchy paths descending from Devil's Tor but the ground is rough and can be very wet above the source of Foxholes Stream. Head towards a clear path that can be seen ascending Rough Tor.
18. Follow the path up Rough Tor from where there is another fine view into central Northern Dartmoor and looking the other way to Haytor and Hameldown ridge. The route now descends to cross the West Dart before returning along the ridge on the opposite side.
19. From Rough Tor continue straight on, following a good path which descends to the West Dart. There may be a second path further left but make sure that you take the one heading due E in the direction of a prominent stone wall and outcrop in the distance. After 0.3 miles this reaches the Dart which can usually be easily crossed on rocks (**6113 7986**).
20. After crossing the river stay on the path heading east. The ruins of **Brown's House** (**6149 7987**) are reached after ~400 yards.

Possibly the most isolated dwelling to be built on Dartmoor since prehistoric times, Brown's House probably stood for no more than two decades. The two roomed single storey stone house was constructed by a Dr Benjamin Brown in 1812. According to Dartmoor legend Mr Brown was not the best looking of men but managed to gain a most attractive young bride. Obsessed with jealousy and perhaps realising his good fortune, Brown would not allow another man to even cast eyes upon his beautiful wife. To keep her safe from other admirers he built the farmhouse on this remote part of Dartmoor. Records show that Dr Brown did build the house after applying to the Duchy of Cornwall for a lease in 1810. Unfortunately he started work on the farm before the lease was granted and the Duchy showed its displeasure by setting the rent at an uneconomic 1s 6d per acre.

Eventually they reduced it to 1s 3d on the condition that Brown built a 2½ mile access road at his own expense. The road was never built and Brown soon sold up. The farm changed hands several times but disappeared from records after 1829, presumably abandoned to the moor.

21. From Brown's House head right (SE) to Lower White Tor ½ mile ahead. There is a path but the first section can be quite boggy. You can soon divert a few yards to visit a **tinners' hut** on the right (**6153 7972**), although this is surrounded by mires.

22. Continue straight on along a path from Lower White Tor to Higher White Tor 0.4 miles ahead (S). A stile over a wall is crossed (**6197 7863**) just before the tor. This is another tor with a good view into central Dartmoor. Fur Tor and Cut Hill can be seen in the distance beyond Rough Tor.

23. Head diagonally right (SW) along a path which descends to Longaford Tor. (Not a path closer to the wall on the right which descends to the Dart.) There is a **stone row** (**6189 7828**) on the left roughly half way between the path and wall, about a third of the way towards Longaford Tor, but it can be difficult to spot.

24. Pass to the left of the massive Longaford Tor (unless you wish to climb the rocks) and continue along the ridge to Littaford Tors. In the Dart valley below is **Wistman's Wood**.

25. Shortly after Littaford Tors the path reaches a stile over a wall (**6159 7671**) after which it forks. Take the right fork which gradually descends towards the Dart, passes through an open gateway in a wall after ½ mile, then joins another track. On one **gatepost** can be seen an iron hanger and on the other the iron slot for the gate's bolt.

26. Follow the track as it descends past Crockern Farm then runs another ~½ mile back to Two Bridges car park.

Higher White Tor Stile

WALK 27

WATERFALL & SANDY HOLE PASS

WALK 27A : ROUNDY PARK CIST, WATERFALL & BEEHIVE HUT : 4 / 5 MILES **

WALK 27B : CONTINUES TO SANDY HOLE PASS : 6 / 7 MILES **

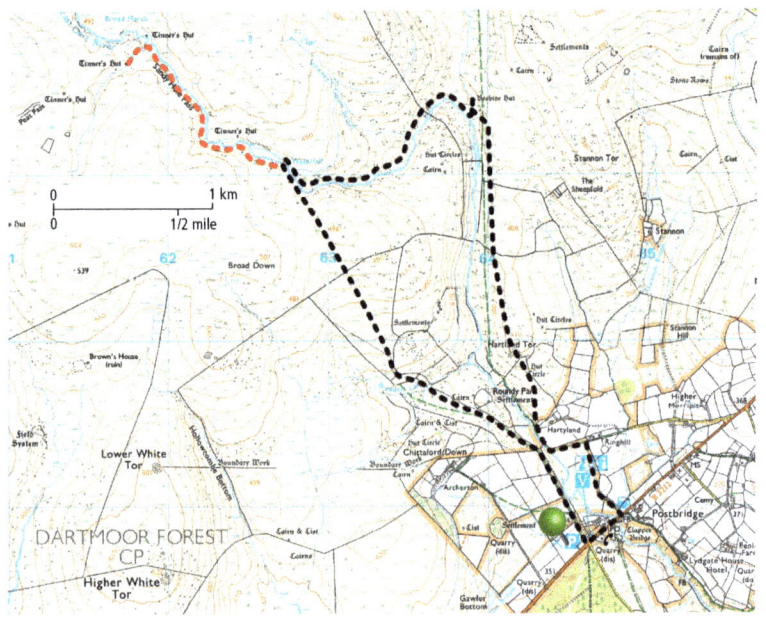

Walk 27A - A walk on paths across open moor to one of Dartmoor's most attractive waterfalls, passing a well preserved burial chamber and tin miners' hut.

Walk 27B continues to an attractive man-made gorge on the River Dart.

Start – Post Bridge car park on B3212 Moretonhampstead to Tavistock road (**647 789**). Charged. Toilets. Visitor centre.

Warnings:

The walks include a number of crossings of streams and rivers. If the East Dart is high do not attempt to cross at Waterfall but return by the outward route (4 / 6 miles).

Walk 27A

1. Take the gravel path which is accessed from either side of the visitor centre and soon crosses a double span **clapper bridge**. This is **Drift Lane**, an ancient route onto the moor.
2. Pass through a gate following the path straight on to the open moor. The East Dart is to the right with Hartland Tor beyond. The path follows the newtake wall as it bends left away from the river. A circular walled pound is soon seen in the field on the right. This is **Roundy Park**.
3. Just outside the far (NE) end of the pound is **Roundy Park Cist** (**6392 7967**). To view this go through a gate ~75 yards beyond the end of the pound and head back diagonally right.

Roundy Park is a Bronze Age pound of roughly 100 metres diameter. Little remains of the hut circles which would have been built inside its wall. The impressive kistvaen is one of the largest on Dartmoor, consisting of seven side slabs (rather than the normal four) and two capstones. It was excavated and restored in 1893 by Robert Barnard, who found two fragments of flint and some burnt bones.

4. Return to the path by the wall which

Roundy Park Cist

East Dart Waterfall

descends to Braddon Lake stream. This can be usually crossed where two channels merge but if necessary there is a ford ~125 yards upstream .

5. Follow a path uphill (initially steep) parallel with the wall, soon reaching a dry leat. This is **Powdermills Leat**.

The high-capacity leat took water from the East Dart to power the three mills at Powder Mills gunpowder factory. This closed in 1897 after demand fell following the invention of dynamite and decline of tin and copper mining.

6. Cross the leat and continue on a path close to the wall, soon passing through a gate. When the path divides after ~200 yards take the left fork which runs ~50 yards from the wall, then bears further left, climbing towards a stile over the wall ahead (***6320 8047***)(just left of rocks).

7. Cross the stile then continue ahead to the summit of the hill (Broad Down), where large rocks lie either side of the path (Broadun Rocks). There is a fine view of East Dart valley and central Northern Dartmoor. The gorge in the East Dart to the left is Sandy Hole Pass and the rocks in the river ahead are Waterfall. Follow the path bending left (NW) to **Waterfall (*6275 8106*)**.

Whilst not the steepest of falls, the curtain of water cascading diagonally over a 7 foot drop, then over ledges to a pool below, makes for a most attractive spot in the shelter of the Dart valley. It is popular location for wild swimming.

8. Walk 27B leaves here. Walk 27A crosses the river which can be achieved at Waterfall if the level is not high. If crossing is problematic return via the outward route (4 miles). Don't take risks.

9. Turn right (SE), following a path on the north bank running not far above the river. Some of this is fairly rough walking. After ~½ mile this crosses Winney's Down Brook and continues above the East Dart, passing above an island divided by a wall.

10. Go through a gate (**6358 8139**) and stay on the path above the Dart as it bends sharp right. On reaching the Lade Hill Brook (not

Beehive Hut

named on OS maps), cross, then follow it upstream for ~100 yards. Here, in an area of mining works, is a **Beehive Hut** (*6393 8145*).

One of the best preserved of the moor's beehive huts, this round stone structure would have been used a tool store for the tinners whose workings can still be seen disturbing the ground around the stream and maybe as a rather cramped shelter from poor weather. There is a good view up the valley to Sittaford Tor.

11. Return towards the Dart and take a path diagonally left (SE) about 60 yards before the river, which climbs gently and soon meets the path from the Grey Wethers stone circle. There is an alternative path closer to the river but this is narrow, passes through gorse and is often muddy. Neither follow the exact route marked on the OS map.

12. Both paths cross two walls before merging and running just below the rocks of Hartland Tor, from where there is a good view of Roundy Park.

13. The path enters a small copse by the Dart and passes through three gates close to the river. After the third gate turn left following a path beside the wall. Turn right where this meets a gate in the wall at the end of the field. It is possible to go diagonally across the field, cutting off a corner, but this is boggy.

14. Follow the path beside the wall until it meets the road by **Post Bridge Clapper**. Turn right on the road for ~175 yards to the car park.

Dartmoor's best-known clapper bridge was first documented in 1655 and may date back as early as the 14th century. It has been repaired many times, the last major work being in 1970 when the stones were adhered with epoxy cement. In the 1820s a local farmer decided to push the slabs into the river to make a pond for his ducks but his plan failed when one of the stones fell flat rather than on its edge.

Walk 27B

15. Follow Walk 27A to Waterfall. Don't cross the Dart but continue upstream on the path close to the river for ~½ mile to **Sandy Hole Pass** (*622 813*).

Sandy Hole Pass

Lying in an area of extensive mining activity, the atmospheric Sandy Hole Pass was formed when tinners straightened, deepened and narrowed the river, increasing its rate of flow. This helped take away the mining waste but caused problems downstream at Dartmouth where sand caused the harbour to silt up.

16. Walk through the pass, then when the gorge opens open take a narrow path diagonally left towards **Broada Stones**, a rocky outcrop just beyond a stream. There is a fine view into central Dartmoor from the rocks.

17. A ruined **Tinners' Hut** (*6173 8166*) can be seen from the rocks, just upstream of the crossing point. After visiting this, recross the stream and head back towards Sandy Hole Pass but take a path running above the gorge rather than through it. This joins your outward path and returns to Waterfall.

18. Options for the return are by the outward route (6 miles), or if safe to cross the Dart at Waterfall, to follow Walk 27A back to Postbridge via the beehive hut (7 miles).

BIBLIOGRAPHY

Dartmoor 365	John Hayward
Dartmoor Atlas of Antiquities	Jeremy Butler
Dartmoor Crosses	F.H. Starkey
Dartmoor Forest Farms	Elisabeth Stanbrook
Dartmoor Sites of Magic & Mystery	John Earle
Dartmoor's Tors and Rocks	Ken Ringwood
Exploring Dartmoor	F.H (Harry) Starkey
Fernworthy An Archaeological Landscape	Dartmoor National Park Authority
Guide to Dartmoor	William Crossing
Merrivale	Dartmoor National Park Authority
Thurlow's Dartmoor Companion	George Thurlow
Walks on Dartmoor Paths and Trackways	Michael Caton
Worth's Dartmoor	R. Hansford Worth
Walking the Dartmoor Railroads	Eric Hemery
Walking the Dartmoor Waterways	Eric Hemery

Various websites, most notably:

www.legendarydartmoor.co.uk
www.dartefacts.co.uk

ALSO BY PETER CATON

50 WALKS ON THE ESSEX COAST
A walking guide covering the entire publicly accessible coast of Essex. Most of the walks have different options with lengths ranging from 2 – 15 miles, catering for both serious ramblers and those looking for just an afternoon stroll.

NO BOAT REQUIRED
EXPLORING TIDAL ISLANDS
Peter sets out to be the first person to visit all of the 43 tidal islands that can be walked to from the UK mainland. He explores islands that few know exist and even fewer have visited, and finds that our tidal islands are special places with many fascinating and amusing stories.

SUFFOLK COAST WALK
Peter explores all 162 miles of Suffolk's unique coastline, describing the route for fellow walkers, with an engaging narrative that tells of the beauty, history and wildlife of this mysterious and varied coast.

ESSEX COAST WALK
A narrative describing Peter's walk along arguably the longest coastline of any English county. With a wealth of information and gentle humour to match the coastline's gentle beauty, the book makes for easy reading.

REMOTE STATIONS
Combining a love of remote places and travelling on our more interesting trains, Peter visits forty of Britain's most lonely railway stations. Most are still in use but a few closed long ago, including two on the Princetown railway.

THE NEXT STATION STOP
FIFTY YEARS BY TRAIN

A 10,000 mile tour of Britain, discovering what it's like to travel on our modern railways and contemplating train journeys made over the last fifty years.

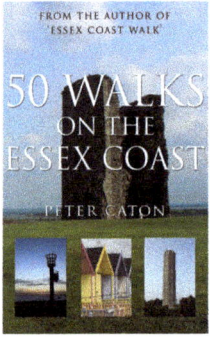
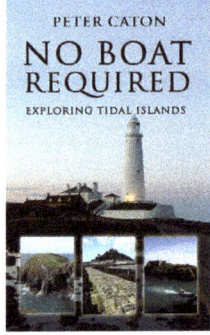
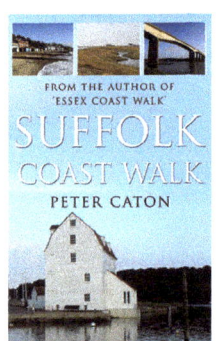
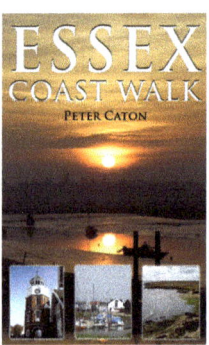
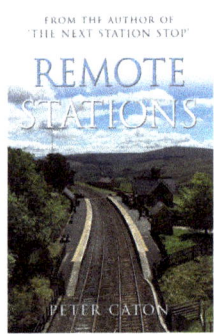
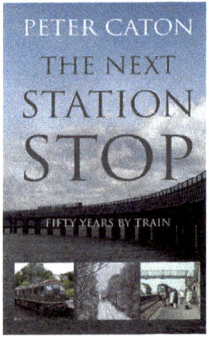

To be published 2024

DARTMOOR ENGLAND'S LAST WILDERNESS?

A Dartmoor narrative, exploring many aspects of the moor by means of a series of varied walks and asking the question, is Dartmoor England's last wilderness?

The author starts by telling us of mishaps he's experienced on Dartmoor and the lessons learned. He moves on to describing walks, each with a theme and including much information on the history, legends, geography and people of the moor. Making use of his father's sixty year old notebooks, he refers back to some of his childhood walks in the 1960s & 70s.

Some of the many controversies and conflicts relating to Dartmoor are discussed, including access, camping and rewilding and the book includes four chapters on battles to save the moor.

The author considers what defines a wilderness, whether Dartmoor qualifies and if so is it England's last. The book could perhaps be described as a Dartmoor miscellany with themes of walks, wilderness, controversies and stories of the moor.

This book is printed on paper from sustainable sources managed under the Forest Stewardship Council (FSC) scheme.

It has been printed in the UK to reduce transportation miles and their impact upon the environment.

For every new title that Troubador publishes, we plant a tree to offset CO_2, partnering with the More Trees scheme.

For more about how Troubador offsets its environmental impact, see www.troubador.co.uk/sustainability-and-community